A Concise History of the Theatre

A Concise History of the Theatre

Phyllis Hartnoll

CHARLES SCRIBNER'S SONS · NEW YORK

3 5 7 9 11 13 15 17 19 I/P 20 18 16 14 12 10 8 6 4 2

Printed in Great Britain
Library of Congress Catalog Card Number 68-27427
ISBN 0-684-13521-3

Contents

CHAPTER ONE

The Greek and Roman Theatre

The origins of the theatre go back far into the past, to the religious rites of the earliest communities. Throughout the history of mankind there can be found traces of songs and dances in honour of a god, performed by priests and worshippers dressed in animal skins, and of a portrayal of his birth, death and resurrection. Even now similar ceremonies can be discovered among primitive peoples. But for the theatre as we understand it today three things are necessary: actors speaking or singing independently of the original unison chorus; an element of conflict conveyed in dialogue; and an audience emotionally involved in the action but not taking part in it. Without these essential elements there may be religious or social ceremonies, but not theatre. It has been argued that the earliest extant Egyptian texts for funerals and coronations, some dating as far back as 3000 B C, are really plays. But an order of service for a coronation in which the king is crowned by the high priest is not a playscript. The event is firmly rooted in reality; and according to Aristotle a play is 'an imitation of an action, and not the action itself'. Even the famous Passion Play of Abydos, which recounts the death, burial and resurrection of the god Osiris, is really a directive for a corporate religious exercise. Before we can talk of theatre we must wait for something a little further removed from reality.

It follows therefore that the first great theatrical age in the history of Western civilization is that of Greece in the fifth century B C. It was there that tragedies and comedies, some of which still exist, were first performed by actors and not by priests, in special buildings or precincts which, though hallowed, were not temples. The ruins of some of these still stand, and provide us with archaeological evidence. There is also some documentation of both performances and buildings, and the influence of both can be traced in the European and American theatre up to the present day.

The origin of the modern theatre can be found in the dithyramb (or unison hymn) sung round the altar of Dionysus, the wine-god whose cult had spread to Greece from the Near East, by a chorus of fifty men, five from each of the ten tribes of Attica. The process of evolution from this simple act of worship to the full-scale Greek tragedy as we find it in classical Athens must have been a slow one, and it is not possible to pinpoint exactly the various stages. But in the earliest plays we find again the fifty members of the chorus, and *Ill. 1* always in the centre of the stage is the altar of Dionysus. The lyric form of the dithyramb accounts for the sung choruses in the play, and its poetic content. Most important of all, the widening of the scope of the dithyramb, which originally dealt only with the life and worship of Dionysus, to include tales of demi-gods or heroes, legendary ancestors of the Greeks and their associate peoples, is reflected in the plays. The deeds of these heroes, good or bad, their wars, feuds, marriages and adulteries, and the destinies of their children, who so often suffered for the sins of their parents, are a source of dramatic tension, and give rise to the essential element of

8

1 (*left*) The Theatre of Dionysus in Athens as it is today. During successive reconstructions it has lost the circular orchestra which survives at Epidaurus (*see Ill. 14*), but the base of the altar of Dionysus can still be seen in the centre of the semicircle

2 (*right*) Greek actor holding a tragic mask and wearing a short chiton and high boots (*cothurni*), from a vase-painting of the late fourth century BC. The mask is that of a strong, handsome hero in the prime of life, with fair hair and beard

conflict – between man and god, good and evil, child and parent, duty and inclination. This may lead to comprehension and reconciliation between the conflicting elements – since a Greek tragedy need not necessarily end unhappily – or to incomprehension and chaos. The plots of all Greek plays were already well known to the audience. They formed part of its religious and cultural heritage, for many of them dated from Homeric times. The interest for the spectator lay, therefore, not in the novelty of the story, but in seeing how the dramatist had chosen to deal with it, and, no doubt, in assessing the quality of the acting, and the work of the chorus, both in singing and dancing, about which unfortunately we know very little.

But Greek drama was not confined to tragedy. Even at its most reverent, the human spirit needs relaxation, and comedy crept in with the revels which took place in the villages when the harvest had been safely gathered in. They were enlivened by the antics of the satyrs – half men, half goats – who were the attendants of Dionysus. It was from their fooling, and from the rough horseplay of other village festivals, that the first true comedies of the theatre developed.

Ill. 3

9

The dithyramb probably continued for some time to extend its scope without achieving any dramatic content. Something, some new element, was needed if worship was to become theatre. And since the natural human reaction to any form of communal activity, when the time comes to catalogue it, is to identify each phase with some recognizable person, it is not surprising that the honour of inaugurating the theatre should be ascribed to one man, Thespis, the leader of a dithyrambic chorus whose name has become synonymous with acting – the 'Thespian art' – just as 'robes of Thespis' means theatrical costume. Thespis is said to have travelled from Icaria, his birthplace, with his chorus, carrying his belongings on a cart whose

Ill. 3 floor and tailboard could form an improvised stage. In the course of his wanderings from one festival to another he eventually reached Athens, and there, as was only right and proper, he was the first to win a prize at the newly established dramatic festival, the City Dionysia.

The great innovation that Thespis made was to detach himself from the chorus and, in the person of the god or hero whose deeds were being celebrated, to engage in dialogue with it. He was thus the first actor as well as the first manager. The step he took was even more revolutionary than it seems to us, for he was the first unsanctified person who dared to assume the character of a god. This had hitherto been the prerogative of the priests or kings, who by virtue of their office were already partly deified. The way was now open for the independent development of the actor and of a building suited to his needs. The early theatres of Greece, like the one at Delphi, for

Ill. 4 instance, were always built near a temple. They continued to be the focal point of a corporate act of worship, but the interpretation of the plays acted in them was entrusted to men who were primarily actors, and only by tradition servants of Dionysus. The spectators too, among whom were some of the former actor-priests, changed. They were still conscious of the religious significance of the play, but they began to judge it as a work of art, and eventually as entertainment, and so became an audience rather than a congregation.

Of the three main festivals of Greece, the Rural Dionysia, held in mid-winter and laying stress on Dionysus as the god of fertility, gave

10

3 The Cart of Thespis, a reconstruction from an Attic vase-painting. Dionysus attended by satyrs is shown on his way to the City Dionysia

to the theatre the leader of the chorus, who was probably the head-man of the village, and also the word for tragedy (from *tragos*, a goat, either because a goat was sacrificed on the first day, or given as a prize on the last). The January festival, the Lenaea, was mainly devoted to merry-making, with elements which contributed to the later development of comedy (the word comes from *comos*, a revel or masquerade). But the festival for which all the extant Greek plays were written, as well as many others which are now lost, was the City Dionysia, celebrated at Athens in April, and attended not only by all able-bodied citizens, but also by official representatives of the federated and allied states. Arrangements began about ten months in advance. Poets who wished to compete had first to submit their works to the presiding officers, who chose three plays for perform-ance. To each poet was then assigned by lot a leading actor, and a patron, or *choregus*, a wealthy man who as part of his civic duties paid all the expenses of the production. The actors were paid by the state. The author of the play composed the music for it, and arranged the dances. Until specialists took over, he also trained the chorus. And until actors increased in numbers and importance he often played the chief part himself.

The first day of the City Dionysia was given over to the splendid procession which is depicted on the frieze of the Parthenon. The actors took part in it, wearing their stage clothes, but without masks. The next three days were devoted to tragedies, and the fourth to comedies, though later on the comedies were given in the evenings, after the tragedies, which began at dawn. Each writer of tragedy had to contribute three plays, either a trilogy on one theme, or three separate plays on a linked theme, and a satyr-play, about which little is known. It seems to have been a bawdy comic comment on the main theme of the tragedies, and was retained as a link with the early worship of Dionysus. Comic dramatists were limited to one play each. A prize was awarded to the best comedy and the best tragedy, to the best production (hence the importance of having a

generous *choregus*) and later to the best tragic actor, who need not necessarily have appeared in the winning play.

Of the many poets who wrote for the City Dionysia, and whose names and play-titles we know from various catalogues compiled in ancient times, the earliest and perhaps the best was Aeschylus. Born in about 525 B C, he was known in his lifetime as a soldier and a citizen as well as a poet. He fought at Marathon and Salamis, and died in 456 B C, while on a visit to Syracuse. He is believed to have written about eighty or ninety plays, of which we have seven complete texts and numerous fragments. His *Oresteia* is the only *Ills. 5, 6* example of a dramatic trilogy which has survived. In his plays we can follow the development of the Greek theatre. In the earliest the chorus still numbers fifty, as in the dithyramb, and there is only one

4 (*left*) The Theatre and Temple of Apollo at Delphi, fourth century B C

5 (*below*) Clytemnestra killing Cassandra, from a vase-painting of *c.* 430 B C. This episode from Aeschylus' *Oresteia* took place off-stage. The costumes probably depict those worn on-stage, both parts being played by men

actor. Later the chorus is reduced to twelve, and a second actor is introduced, followed eventually by a third. All Aeschylus' plays are powerful, majestic, and written in superb verse. After his death they were often revived, though normally only new plays were given at the festival, and they are still well-known and often acted in translation, particularly the first part of the *Oresteia*, which deals with the murder of Agamemnon by his wife Clytemnestra.

The next well-known dramatist of Athens was Sophocles, who was younger than Aeschylus and of a very different temperament. His most productive period of playwriting coincided with the finest phase of Athenian history, under Pericles. He too wrote about ninety plays, of which seven survive, and won eighteen prizes, always the first or second, never the third. His last play, *Oedipus at Colonus*, a sequel to the better known *Oedipus the King*, which has often been *Ill. 262* revived in the modern theatre, was written at the end of his long life – he was ninety when he died – and produced posthumously. Sophocles, who was of a serene and well-balanced disposition, handsome, successful and highly esteemed by his contemporaries, was a less powerful writer than Aeschylus, whose themes were cosmic, but more humane, more closely concerned with the complexities of human relationships as opposed to those of gods and men. His plots are more complex, his characterization, as in his *Antigone* and *Electra*, more subtle, his lyrics more flexible and harmonious. Greek tragedy, in his plays, is moving away from the simplicity and severity of its origins, and the chorus, which he increased from twelve to fifteen, probably for some technical reason connected with the pattern of the choral dances, is less closely integrated into the action.

The innovations of Sophocles were continued by his younger contemporary Euripides, the last great writer of Greek tragedy. Born in about 484 BC, he died in 406, the same year as Sophocles. He was a man of good family, something of a recluse, and more of an individualist than either of his predecessors. Among his plays, of which eighteen survive out of a possible ninety-two, is the *Cyclops*, the only complete satyr-play which we now have. Sceptical, modern in outlook, and as he got older, increasingly outspoken, Euripides was evidently less popular in his own day than Aeschylus and

6 Apollo protecting Orestes from the Furies, a scene from Aeschylus' *Oresteia*, shown in a vase-painting of *c.* 370

Sophocles, winning a prize only five times. His plays were more easily understood and appreciated by later generations, which may account for the number that have survived, and they are still popular today. They are unusually realistic, no longer pure tragedies, but tragi-comedies, even melodramas. Several of them are studies of abnormal states of mind, and he was interested in problems of feminine psychology. Among his innovations was the use of the prologue, in the modern sense of the word, to summarize the situation at the opening of the play. He also accelerated the process by which the chorus became less and less important. In some of his plays – the *Medea*, for instance, and the *Hippolytus* – which deal with the emotions of individuals rather than the great public events debated in earlier tragedies, he must have found the chorus an encumbrance, and his successors tended to dispense with it altogether, using a vestigial group of singers and dancers to break up the action with independent interludes.

While tragedy was developing in the hands of these three dramatists, the various forms of comedy fused to produce the plays of Aristophanes, who was born in 448 BC and died in 380. He is the only comic dramatist of Athens of whom we have complete plays; of others we have only fragments. But, like Shakespeare, he seems to embody in himself half a dozen writers. Much of his comedy is ephemeral and closely related to the politics and social customs of his own day. The best of it defies translation. Yet so strong is the tradition of his genius that his name is used as a label for bawdy, topical and sophisticated comedy in all countries. We have eleven of the forty plays which he is known to have written, and many of them take their titles from the disguises assumed by the chorus –
Ill. 7   *Knights, Wasps, Birds, Clouds, Frogs.* And it is mainly through the chorus that the author's satire is conveyed. The basic idea in each play is comic in itself, and is reinforced by a series of loosely-connected incidents which give full scope to the inventiveness of both author and actor, for here, as always in comedy, the actor contributed much to the final effect. No modern writer could hope to get away with the invective, social satire, personal criticism, buffoonery and obscenity of the bulk of Aristophanes' work. In translation the wit and savagery tend to evaporate. A modern audience knows too little about the background to be able to appreciate the topical allusions. All that can be done is to stress the universal as opposed to the contemporary aspects of the play, perhaps with discreet modernization of some incidents. In this way most of the plays have been revived, notably the *Birds* and the *Frogs* in modern Greek by the Greek Art Theatre under Karolos Koun.

The actors in Greek tragedy, whose costumes we know mainly from Greek vase-paintings of theatrical scenes, wore elaborate
Ills. 5, 6   robes, often brightly coloured and heavily embroidered, and high
Ill. 2   boots (*cothurni*) in imitation of their god, Dionysus. Later their robes
Ill. 23   were padded and their height increased by a head-dress (*onkos*) and by thick soles under the boots. This, in the vast open-air theatres of the time, gave them an impressive dignity suitable to the characters they portrayed and enhanced their stage presence. The most important feature of their costume was the mask, said to have been intro-

16

duced by Thespis. In light wood, cork or linen, this enabled the three *Ills. 2, 11, 23*
actors in a tragedy to play several parts each, and also, in a theatre
staffed entirely by men, to impersonate women. Each mask – more
than thirty types are known to have existed – indicated not only the
age, standing and sex of the character, but the dominant emotion –
fear, rage, hate, despair. The actor, denied the use of facial expression
and limited by his costume to broad sweeping gestures, was forced
to rely on the range and expressiveness of his voice for most of his
effects. Even after the reforms of Euripides – who was criticized by

7 Actors dressed as birds, from a vase-painting of *c.* 500 BC. Although earlier than
Aristophanes' comedy, this scene may indicate how the chorus in his *Birds* was
dressed. The costume perpetuates the traditional use of animal disguises in early
religious ceremonies

8 (*left*) Hellenistic statuette of a comic actor wearing a mask, from Tralles in Turkey

9 (*above*) Archaic Punic comic mask from Tunis

10 (*right*) Hellenistic comic mask from Athens

11 (*far right*) A marble replica of the mask of a tragic heroine. This is a late Roman example of the 'fair, long-haired, tragic heroine' but is probably modelled on earlier Greek masks

Aristophanes in one of his comedies for dressing his actors 'in rags' – the Greek tragic actor remained a static, godlike creature, speaking and singing in harmony with specially composed music, all of which is lost, and sinking his individuality in the character he portrayed. The chorus, who needed more freedom of movement, wore the dress of the people they represented, and light masks.

The costume of the comic actor was, as might be expected, less hampering, since he needed to be something of an acrobat. He usually wore soft slippers (*socci*), flesh-coloured tights, a short tunic, *Ills. 12, 13* grotesquely padded, and in the comedies of the time of Aristophanes, *Ill. 10* a large red leather phallus. Masks were exaggerated for comic effect. The attendants of Dionysus in the satyr-play wore short furry breeches to which were attached a tail and a phallus.

18

12–13 (*right*) Actors in Old Comedy, statuettes of the mid-fourth century BC. On▶ the left, a slave who is pretending to be deaf, or who has just received a box on the ear; right, two drunken slaves or revellers, wearing tights, padded jackets and the phallus

Of the theatres in which the Greek plays were first performed little survives, but it is possible to reconstruct the essential details, either from later buildings, or from the architectural evidence of the Theatre of Dionysus in Athens, which has several times been *Ill. 1* remodelled. The heart of the theatre was the original dancing-place, the flat circular space with the altar of Dionysus in the centre which was used by the chorus. This orchestra, as it was called, is admirably *Ill. 14* preserved in the theatre at Epidaurus, which is still used for an annual summer dramatic festival. The musicians probably sat or

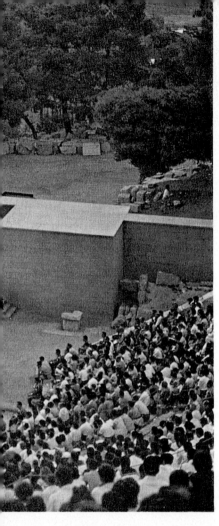

14 A modern performance in the restored theatre at Epidaurus, showing its steep auditorium and well-preserved orchestra

stood on the altar steps. In a horseshoe shape round the orchestra, on rising ground, sat the audience, first on the bare hill-side, later on wooden benches, later still on stone or marble seats. In the centre of the front row were the elaborate stone seats reserved for the priest of Dionysus, to whom the god himself appeals for help in Aristophanes' *Frogs*, and other high officials and state visitors. Entrance was at first free. Later a small charge was made. Poor citizens were then given the necessary entrance money, since attendance at the City Dionysia was practically compulsory.

Behind the orchestra there was, probably from very early times, a stage building reminiscent of the front of the original temple. It served the practical purpose of providing the actors with a background and a sounding-board, and of concealing the dressing-rooms, the stage machinery and such properties as might be needed – the red carpet in the *Agamemnon*, the head of Pentheus in the *Bacchae*, Hector's shield in the *Trojan Women*. It was pierced by a large central double door with a smaller door on each side, by which the actors came and went. The chorus entered along two passages between the stage building and the auditorium which could also be used by the audience as it assembled. The most important part of the stage machinery was the crane (*machine*) by which the god could descend from heaven to sort out the complications of the plot (whence the expression *deus ex machina*), but there was also a wheeled platform on which a pre-arranged tableau could be shown, and a machine for imitating thunder. There was no scenery in the modern sense of the word, but the stage wall provided an increasingly elaborate architectural background, and on each side of the stage were the *periaktoi*. These were triangular prisms which could be rotated to indicate symbolically a change of scene by means of a painted tree, a column, or waves.

It seems reasonable to suppose, in view of the size of the theatres, that there was, in front of the stage building and behind the orchestra, a raised platform for the actors, to make them easier to see, and to single them out from the chorus. Certainly in later times there was *Ill. 1* quite a high stage, with a marble frieze below and a short flight of steps up from the orchestra.

By the time the great stone buildings which we think of as typically Greek were in use, the control of the theatre had passed from the dramatists to the actors, as happened frequently in later theatre history, and the great days of Greek drama were over. Comedy was *Ill. 15* paramount, but the only writer of note was Menander, who was born about 342 BC and died in 292. Only five of his plays have survived, and these are incomplete, but he had an immense reputation in antiquity, and enough fragments of his work remain to enable us to assess the main features of his 'New Comedy', as it was called, to

15 Menander in his studio with New Comedy masks, from a relief now in Rome. The masks are those of three of Menander's chief characters: a young man, a courtesan and an angry father. The girl on the right, who is perhaps holding another mask, may be the Muse of Comedy, or Menander's mistress, Glykera

16 A scene from a Roman comedy, before AD 79, from a Pompeiian wall-painting. It appears to depict a jeering slave who has surprised a pair of lovers

17 The Roman theatre at Sabratha, the largest in North Africa. Built about AD 200, this has the typical Roman semicircular orchestra, raised stage and elaborate three-storey *frons scaenae*

distinguish it from the Old Comedy of Aristophanes. It is markedly different, being pleasantly humorous, politically inoffensive, dealing superficially with comic situations of contemporary urban life, and hardly satiric at all, though still bawdy. Its fabricated plots tell of family matters, missing children, delayed marriages, mislaid treasure, *Ills. 18, 19* in all of which the wily and astute slave plays a leading part. It is, in fact, a romantic comedy of manners which has lost all traces of its religious origins, and in which the chorus no longer has a place.

It was this type of Greek comedy, played in the vast Hellenistic theatres with their high stages and elaborate scene-buildings, which the Romans came into contact with as they extended their empire southwards into Greece. Easily understood and assimilated, it was *Ill. 16* imported into Italy, where it underwent some significant changes, and gave rise to the works of the two main writers of Roman comedy

24

18–19 (*right*) Actors in New Comedy, probably characters in plays based on, though not necessarily by, Menander. The statuette on the left represents a potter or drinker, the one on the right a money-lender or dealer, or a thieving slave

20 A scene from Terence's *Adelphi*, in a later copy of a fourth- or fifth-century original. It shows Aeschinus and his brother Ctesipho confronted by the slave-dealer Sannio (led by their slave Syrus) from whom they have stolen a girl Ctesipho loves

(*fabula palliata*), Plautus and Terence. From it they took their plots and many of the stock characters, the irascible old men, the young profligates, the officious slaves, who make up the *dramatis personae* of their plays.

Plautus, of whose plays twenty survive, was primarily a translator and adaptor, basing his comedies on Greek originals now lost, but transferring the action to Rome and introducing recognizable details of Roman life and manners. His characters are sharply differentiated types. Among them can be found the braggart soldier (*miles gloriosus*), the miser, the parasite, the identical twins (whose adventures provided Shakespeare with the material for his *Comedy of Errors*), and always the browbeaten but resourceful slave whose actions provide the mainspring of most of the comedies. Plautus was an excellent craftsman, and his plays act better than they read. Terence, a freed slave from Africa, had more originality and was a better writer, since, owing to the kindness of an aristocratic patron, he was better educated. In his plays, of which six survive, there are *Ill. 20* fewer topical allusions and less buffoonery than in Plautus, and the application of his plots and dialogue is more universal. Perhaps for these reasons they became unpopular with audiences whose taste ran more to rope dancing, gladiators, and players of pantomine. But like Seneca, whose tragedies were written to be read and not for the stage, both Plautus and Terence were destined to have an enormous influence on the dramatists of a much later and far different age from their own.

While the written comedies of Plautus and Terence languished for lack of audiences, the short rustic farce of southern Italy, the *fabula atellana*, gained in popularity. Its appeal was based on the purely Roman humour of the clowns Maccus and Bucco, the foolish old man Pappus, and the hunchbacked slave Dossennus. Imported into Rome, it abandoned the use of dialect, and replaced its impromptu plots by formal written texts, of which a few titles survive. In the form in which it flourished under the dictatorship of Sulla it provided the only truly indigenous type of Roman drama. It evidently had very little literary value, and its appeal was immediate and ephemeral. But it deserves to be mentioned because of the curious parallels

26

21 A Roman mime play, before AD 79, showing the elaborately built-up stage
with three entrances and an upper storey. On stage, a young hero, two warriors,
and two slaves at the rear, one with a torch, the other with a wine-jar, evidently
making preparations for a feast

it presents to the early manifestations of the later Italian popular
drama, the *commedia dell'arte* (see Chapter 3).

The theatres of the Roman world were very different from those
of Greece. They were built on flat ground, not on a hillside, with a
vast surrounding wall of masonry, often elaborately decorated. *Ill. 17*
With the disappearance of the chorus the last link with the dithyramb
had been severed, and the orchestra was no longer needed. The focal
point of the Roman theatre building was therefore the high stage,
with tiers of benches in front and an elaborate stage wall, the *frons* *Ill. 21*
scaenae, behind, often two storeys high. This stage had obvious
affinities with the primitive temporary platforms – the *phlyakes* stages

27

22 On a *phlyakes* stage with supporting pillars and a side entrance (*see also Ill. 20*), a miser, Charinus, is trying to protect his treasure-chest from thieves. A vase-painting of the mid-fourth century B C. It was probably from temporary stages like this that the typical Roman stage (*see Ill. 17*) developed

Ill. 22

– on which farcical mime-plays had been performed in southern Italy up to about 300 B C. One can see from the many extant vase-paintings of *phlyakes* performances how the high platform with panels or curtains developed, and also how grotesquely costumed and exaggeratedly comic the mime-players were in the travesties of Greek tragedy or in the plays based on the amorous adventures of Zeus and the Seven Labours of Hercules which made up much of their repertory.

By the first centuries of the new era Roman theatres had been built all over Italy, in Spain and France, and in the colonies of North Africa. Some of them are still in an excellent state of preservation and

23 Tragic actor with mask, showing the high wig (*onkos*), a wall-painting from Herculaneum, therefore before A D 79. Judging by his untidy hair, the seated actor has just taken off his tragic mask, which can be seen on the far right. The man at the back is probably his dresser

one can see how imposing they must have been when they were newly built. They had every embellishment, including a curtain which disappeared into a trough at the front of the stage. For the spectators there were awnings, fruit-sellers and, on hot days, showers of perfumed water. But they were beautiful empty shells, housing a dying art. The performances seen in them could not compare with those in the simple wooden buildings of early Greek times. Their staple fare was bawdy and obscene mimes and farces dealing mainly with drunkenness, greed, adultery and horseplay, or lavish acrobatic spectacles featuring scantily clad dancers. Actors, who in Greece had been citizens of good repute, were no longer esteemed. Roscius,

Ill. 17

Ill. 24

whose name has become synonymous with good acting, was perhaps an honourable exception, but even Cicero, who defended him in a lawsuit, thought of drama as something to be read. Theatrical performances, once the glory of Greece, and of some importance even in Republican Rome, became under the Empire little more than a vulgar form of popular entertainment. The time came when they were forbidden altogether. Forgetful of its religious origins and its glorious past, the theatre, as so often in its history, seemed to die of its own inanity, only to revive, more strongly than ever, in an unexpected direction.

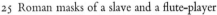

24 (*left*) 'Bikini'-clad girls dancing in a Roman aquatic spectacle, from a mosaic of the late third century A D. 'Water-ballets' were very popular with Roman audiences, and for these, and for the production of *naumachiae* (mock sea-battles), the orchestra – even that of the Theatre of Dionysus in Athens (*see Ill. 1*) – was sealed round and flooded

25 Roman masks of a slave and a flute-player

CHAPTER TWO

The Medieval Theatre

Throughout the history of the theatre there is nowhere to be found a complete break in continuity of development. Between the decay of one form of theatrical presentation and the rise of another, however different, there must always have been some connection, some current flowing, however far underground, to convey the fundamentals of the art from one era to another. After the disappearance of classical drama came the age of the liturgical or church drama of western Europe. It was for a long time thought that there was no connection between the two; that one died with the invasion of the barbarians and that after a gap of several centuries the other was born. This is to underestimate both the force of the mimetic instinct in man and the stubbornness of inherited traditions. The Dark Ages were perhaps not so dark after all, theatrically speaking.

It is true that the later Roman theatre had no great dramatists. Plays were read and quoted from, but not acted. Even the famous nun of Gandersheim, Hroswitha, who in the tenth century took Terence as a model for her dramatized lives of saintly women, may not have written with performance in mind. But we know, on the evidence of manuscript illustrations, that certainly the plays of Terence, and probably those of other writers, were often read aloud *Ill. 28* while actors mimed the story. Meanwhile, the humbler entertainers of the classical world wandered across Europe, alone or in small *Ills. 26, 27* groups. Among them were acrobats, dancers, mimics, animal-trainers with bears or monkeys, jugglers, wrestlers, ballad-singers, story-tellers. Carrying with them the germ of the theatre, ready to take root again when conditions proved favourable, they lived as best they could and handed on the skills and technical tricks bequeathed to them by earlier generations of mime-players. Their existence is proved by the attacks made on them by the more austere Fathers of the Church, attacks which contributed not a little to the

32

26 Medieval entertainers in fools' dress, similar to that of the Roman fools and court jesters; an illuminated manuscript of *c.* 1340 from Flanders

decay of the classical tradition, since from earliest times Christians were strictly forbidden to attend theatrical performances or to appear in them. Yet in Byzantium, it seems, efforts were made to adapt the old pagan theatre to the needs of the new religion, and there are traces of religious plays being performed for the edification of the faithful, perhaps under the influence of the Empress Theodora, *Ill. 29* who was a mime-player before she married Justinian. Slight though the traces of this Christianized theatre are, they exist, and must be remembered when we consider the widespread development of the new liturgical drama. Even if we remain faithful to the conventional view of the latter's origins, we must not overlook the possibility of

27 A medieval glove-puppet booth, *c.* 1340, from the same manuscript

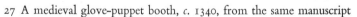

29 (*right*) A contemporary mosaic portrait of the sixth-century Byzantine Empress Theodora, formerly an actress, from San Vitale, Ravenna. Her husband Justinian published an edict permitting a nobleman to marry an actress provided she renounced her profession

the influence on it, even as late as the twelfth or thirteenth century, of the Byzantine theatre of the ninth or tenth.

It is in any case sufficiently ironic that the drama, so strictly forbidden to Christians – often by men who, like St Augustine, had enjoyed it before their conversion – should renew itself in the very heart of their cult. Just as Greek drama developed from the worship of Dionysus, so medieval liturgical drama developed from the Christian liturgy, particularly from the Easter celebrations, since the Resurrection, far more than the Nativity, was the focal point of the Christian year. The process was a slow one, and uneven. In some places the Church was more experimental, in others more conservative. But in general a clear pattern emerges, showing a definite progress from a simple act of faith in a ritual setting to a full-scale pageant on the life of Christ, acted in Latin and utilizing the whole of the church building. With the introduction of the vernacular, and the removal of the performance to an area outside the church, the way was open for the growth of a national theatre in each country. But as long as Latin remained the universal language of Christendom, the liturgical or ecclesiastical play continued to be the chief means of religious instruction for a largely illiterate population.

Ills. 30–2

◀ 28 (*left*) A play by Terence being read and mimed; below he is seen presenting his book to a patron; from a manuscript of *c.* 1400

Like the dithyramb, the lyrical portion of the Easter morning service provided the germ of future developments. There were, in early Christian festivals, sung portions known as *tropes*. The *trope* for Easter consisted of a short dialogue, together with some rudimentary stage directions. It is known from its opening words as the '*Quem quaeritis*' – 'Whom seek ye?'. This was sung by a priest in a white robe, representing the angel at the empty tomb, to three choirboys representing the three Marys who visited it on the first Easter morning – 'Whom seek ye in the sepulchre, O children of Christ?' To which they replied, 'Jesus of Nazareth the crucified, O child of Heaven.' 'He is not here, He has risen again as He foretold. Go,

Ill. 31

Ill. 30

36

30 (*far left*) The Three Marys at the Tomb, from a manuscript of *c.* 980. This illustrates the Easter *trope* shown in *Ill. 31*, and antedates the liturgical drama, being no doubt based on the scene during the Easter Mass when three choirboys approached the shrine or hollow side-altar from which the cross deposited there on Good Friday had been removed

31 (*left*) The Easter *trope* '*Quem quaeritis?*' ('Whom seek ye?'), from which European liturgical drama developed; from a Dublin Sarum Processional of the fourteenth century. The stage direction at the top of this extract instructs the Angel of the Resurrection to appear and speak to the women

32 (*right*) An alabaster plaque of the Resurrection from Nottingham, showing the Risen Christ and three soldiers asleep, a scene very probably inspired by a liturgical drama

announce that He is risen from the dead.' Then priest and choirboys, turning to the congregation, led them in a joyful Easter hymn.

It is impossible to chart the theatre's progress accurately, or to assign developments to any particular place. Liturgical plays are found all over Europe. The Mystery plays of England, the *mystères* of France, the *sacre rappresentazioni* of Italy, the *autos sacramentales* of Spain, the *Geistspiele* of the German-speaking lands, as well as the scattered examples from central and eastern Europe, all have in common their theme and the assumption of devotion and belief in their audiences. And just as the dithyramb was expanded to include stories of gods and heroes, so the simple scene of the three Marys at the

37

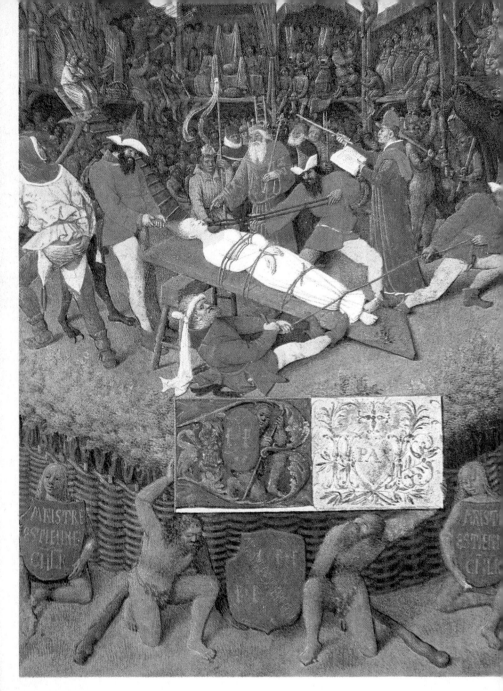

34 The Annunciation, the Nativity and the Resurrection, from Wakefield, Yorkshire. Wakefield is known to have had a long tradition of liturgical acting, and it
is reasonable to suppose that these scenes approximate to what was seen on-stage

◀ 33 A French open-air performance of a religious drama, *Le Martyre de S. Apolline*,
c. 1460, from a miniature by Jehan Fouquet. It shows a raised, fixed stage with
simultaneous décor of six 'houses'. A ladder connects Heaven with the *platea*, or
playing-place, and Hell has two storeys, with the devils above and Hell-Mouth
below. The man with a book and a wand is the producer

tomb was enlarged by the addition of earlier and later scenes taken
from the Bible, working forward to the Resurrection and eventually *Ills. 32, 34*
to the Second Coming, and backward beyond the Crucifixion and *Ill. 42*
the Trial of Jesus to the Nativity, and so to the prophets of the Old *Ill. 34*
Testament who foretold His coming. From the great storehouse of
literature represented by the Bible were taken also such dramatic
stories as that of Noah's Ark, Jonah and the Whale, Daniel in the
Lion's Den, Samson and Delilah, and many others. And when they
had exhausted the Bible, writers turned to the stories of saints and
martyrs. Some of these told of saints whose conversion had taken *Ill. 33*
place while they were acting in obscene burlesques designed to
ridicule the new religion, and these provide interesting information
on the last days of the Roman theatre.

The first liturgical plays were written for performance by priests and choirboys in a church. As more incidents were added, laymen were allowed to appear, though not as yet any women. More space was needed as the cast list grew longer and the actors took over areas formerly occupied by the congregation. The lay-out of the acting area, whether the play was being done in a small church or in a vast cathedral, was roughly the same. The altar with its crucifix was the central point. On its right (from the priest's point of view as he faced the congregation) was Heaven, on its left Hell. The prophets spoke their lines from the pulpit. On each side of the central nave were the sites needed for the scenes in the play. They might include *Ill. 36* Bethlehem, Nazareth, Herod's palace, the Temple at Jerusalem, with *Ill. 35* the money-changers, the house of Caiaphas and the palace of *Ill. 42* Pilate, the Mount of Olives, Gethsemane, Golgotha and the tomb of the Resurrection. These sites had many names – mansions, houses and booths were some of them. The space between was the unlocalized 'playing-place' (the *platea*) which was to persist for hundreds of years and to prove so useful to future dramatists like Shakespeare, since it could represent any place the writer chose to make it. The whole church thus provided a multiple setting in which all the scenes needed for a performance were in full view of the audience all the time.

It is not known how soon the rapidly developing new drama moved out of the church. One reason for its removal may have been overcrowding; another the license and bawdry that crept in. In some places it was ejected as soon as its original simplicity had been lost; in others it lingered on until the sixteenth century. The twelfth-century Anglo-Norman play *Adam*, one of the earliest to include speeches in the vernacular, was certainly set out of doors, with the church doors forming a background through which God and the chief actors came and went, while the devils ran about in front of the raised platform. In Spain, on the other hand, the first reference to a religious play which was acted in a nobleman's hall and not in a church dates from the mid-fifteenth century. Long before that time the religious play was fully developed. It was as cosmic as anything by Aeschylus, and as much a part of its audience's life. Scepticism had

40

no doubt crept in, as it had done in Athens with Euripides. But by that time the simple restatement of a known truth had become a conscious and complex work of art.

There were two ways of presenting the innumerable small scenes which made up the play-cycles, of which four or five are known in England and many more on the Continent. The first method was static, the second perambulating. In the first the 'houses' were arranged in a semicircle, as in the play of St Apollonia, or in a straight line, as at the Valenciennes play, with the audience in front. *Ill. 33* There was also an early form of theatre-in-the-round, with the *Ill. 36* 'houses' grouped round a central space, and the audience on raised tiers all round. This method of production was evidently used in Cornwall, where the remains of similar amphitheatres can still be seen. In each case the action progressed from one 'house' to another as the script demanded. It will be seen from the settings of the St Apollonia and Valenciennes plays that Heaven is still on the actor's right and Hell on his left.

35 Christ driving out the money-changers from the Temple, a scene from a fifteenth-century Passion Play performed in St Stephen's Church, Vienna. This scene, with its opportunities for violence and horse-play, is found in several liturgical dramas

36 (*above*) The setting for the Valenciennes Passion Play, 1547. Here the 'houses' are more numerous than in the *S. Apolline* (*Ill. 33*) and are arranged in a straight line. In addition to Hell-Mouth there is a torture-chamber and a lake for St Peter

Le limbe des peres

Lenfer

La porte doree

Maison des euesques

La mer

37 (below) The Triumph of Isabella, Brussels, 1615, including pageants of the Annunciation (centre middle-ground), followed by Diana and her Nymphs, and the Nativity (centre, left-hand page), with an angel perched on the roof

But sometimes – and this is particularly true of England – each scene in the production was mounted on a two-storey 'pageant' or cart, like those used in royal processions and triumphal entries, and a succession of such carts then paraded round the town. The actors repeated the play at each stopping-place in front of a group of spectators who remained where they were to await the next pageant. When plays were no longer acted in churches they were taken over by the secular authorities, and by the trade guilds. This arrangement of the different scenes on carts made possible a division of labour by which each guild assumed the responsibility for a particular scene, usually one connected with its work. Noah's Ark was staged by the shipwrights, the Tower of Babel by the carpenters, Jonah and the Whale by the fishmongers, and so on.

The religious content of the liturgical plays (or Bible-histories, as they are now called) need not be stressed. The Christian story is part of the heritage of Western civilization. One feature remains to be considered, however, and that is the comic element. It is important in the development of the theatre because it was the interpolation of

Ill. 37

39 (*above*) Medieval devil's mask from the Tyrol, an animal head with curved horns and ass's ears

38 (*left*) Christ's Descent into Hell, showing the influence on the early sixteenth-century Flemish painter (school of Hieronymus Bosch) of the stage portrayal of Hell-Mouth (*see Ills. 33 and 36*)

comic scenes which did not appear in the original stories that led to the use of the vernacular. And this in its turn was the chief factor in the emergence of a national theatre in each separate country of Europe.

Greek tragedy, though it may have had touches of humour, more in the acting perhaps than in the text, reserved its buffoonery for the traditional satyr-play which followed. But almost from the beginning the medieval play, which was a tragedy with a happy ending, fused the two together. In the Easter play the first comic characters to be introduced were the merchants at whose shop the Marys stopped on their way to the tomb to buy the spices needed for the embalming of Christ's body. In the Christmas play it was easy to introduce comic characters among the shepherds. One of the best known is Mak the Sheepstealer, from the Chester cycle. Noah's wife became a shrew, the workmen at the Tower of Babel were given comic dialogue, Herod 'raged' amusingly when he heard of the Christ-Child's escape from the massacre of the Innocents. And always the greatest comic character was Satan himself, with his attendant devils, who after the

Ills. 33, 36, 38

45

scene of the Last Judgment gleefully shovelled the lost souls into Hell-Mouth. These devils were also allowed to intrude into many scenes where they had no business to be, simply in order to satisfy the popular demand for comic byplay. They wore masks as horrifying as any of the classical masks, and they probably provided interludes of acrobatic dancing and farcical miming between the scenes.

Ills. 39, 41

A link with the theatre's distant past can perhaps be found in these comic characters. The Byzantine theatre could have passed on to the actor-priests something of the traditions of classical acting, but it is surely from among the wandering entertainers that the players of comedy were drawn. Nor was that all. Someone must have had to direct the liturgical play. Amateurs with clear voices and good memories might do well enough in the serious parts, but as the plays grew more complex even they would feel the need for guidance. So would the crowds of soldiers and townsfolk. The devils too would have needed a variety of skills beyond the scope of most amateurs, and a restraining hand if their fooling was not to become tiresome. The medieval theatre has sometimes been called primitive, even simple. If there was simplicity, it must have been in the early days, when the congregation was linked in worship with the priestly actors. There was nothing simple about the play once it escaped from the church, or even before. To judge by the stage directions in the extant texts, the performances must have been extremely complicated, and they demanded a vast number of properties and working machinery. The raised wooden platform stage concealed traps, there were cranes by which God and his angels could descend from Heaven, and in the Mons play of 1501 the mechanism of Hell-Mouth, which opened to belch out clouds of smoke and closed to swallow up the damned, was so complicated that it took seventeen men to work it. The stage carpenters thought nothing of producing floods, fires, and earthquakes. Realistic executions were called for, with bloody wounds, severed heads and limbs. There was plenty of scope for livestock – rabbits, sheep, a ram for sacrifice, asses for Balaam and for the Flight into Egypt. Costumes were elaborate, and sometimes splendidly embroidered. Leather provided supple suits for the devils, breeches for the men, gloves for God. There was a profusion of

Ill. 40

46

40 The Three Wise Men, from a sixteenth-century Flemish Nativity Play, carrying incense, gold and myrrh. There is a slight suggestion of the Orient in their head-dresses and flowing robes

jewellery. There were gilded haloes, and for God and the archangels gilded masks. There was also the instrumental or vocal music, performed by gaily dressed groups. All of this combined to produce a moving, colourful spectacle set against painted 'houses' to which the deep red or black costumes of the devils lent sombre undertones. *Ill. 41* It is not surprising that the miniature depicting the play of Saint Apollonia shows on the stage a functionary who appears to be *Ill. 33* directing a rehearsal, or even a performance, with the help of a prompt-book and a long wand.

41 Two medieval devils, (*left*) Devil Bell and (*right*) Astaroth; pen drawings from a manuscript of 1539, Zurich. The elaborate costumes, with horns, tails and animal masks, can also be seen on the devils in *Ills. 33* and *36*

The Bible-history, and the later play of abstract vice and virtue, the Morality play, of which *Everyman* is the supreme example, made up the official theatre of the Middle Ages. Performances of a complete cycle of Biblical plays might take place under the auspices of the civic authorities every four, five or ten years, while selected scenes could be done more often. The subject-matter was Christian, but traces of the architectural background of the classical theatre can be found in the construction of the outdoor stage with its aligned 'houses', in the use of masks and machinery, and particularly in the imported comic and bawdy elements. There is also the less tangible but still perceptible feeling of theatrical traditions and experience, handed on, garbled perhaps but still valid, through generations of wandering players. The plays themselves were often extremely well written, exciting and dramatic. The audience was accustomed to pass rapidly through the whole gamut of emotions. In quick succession they experienced the wonder of Creation, the humour of Noah's wife, the curious predicament of Jonah, the tenderness of the Nati-

Ill. 34   vity, the savagery of the massacre of the Innocents, the tragedy of the

42 Scenes from the Valenciennes Passion Play, 1547 (*see also Ill. 36*), from the Carrying of the Cross to the Deposition in the Tomb – the latter a sarcophagus which, unlike the one shown in *Ill. 30*, is large enough to contain the actor until the moment of the Resurrection

Crucifixion, the joy of the Resurrection, and the solemnity of the Ills. 32, 34, 42
Last Judgment. When a national drama finally developed, the
audience in each country, conditioned by the liturgical play, was
ready to receive whatever the dramatists might have to offer.

These old plays can still be successful in production. This has been
proved by the revival of the York cycle in front of York Minster, of
the Wakefield cycle at the Mermaid Theatre in London, of *The Play
of Daniel* by an American company on tour, and by the Polish Resurrection play seen at the Aldwych in London in 1967. There is no
unbroken tradition of liturgical play-production. The Bible-history
died out in most European countries under the impact of the Renaissance and the Reformation. Even the famous Passion Play at Ober-
ammergau is a late revival. Everything has to be rediscovered. But it
often proves well worth discovering, and the plays reveal in production more links than one might have supposed with what went
before and what is to come after.

While the vast liturgical plays were extending their range, and
attracting to themselves whatever there was of theatrical talent in the

43 A scene from *Maître Pierre Pathelin*, c. 1465, the most famous of all medieval
French farces. The rascally lawyer Pathelin, who has defrauded a shopkeeper,
Guillaume, of a length of cloth, pretends to be dying, while his wife Guillemette
parleys with Guillaume at the door

larger centres of population, there was also a continuous thread of secular drama. To this tradition belong the Mayday games and the Mumming plays in rural England, the *soties* or 'tomfooleries' which began with the French Feast of Fools, the farces of the student companies, of which the most famous is *Maître Pierre Pathelin*, the comic interludes of the German *Meistersinger*, the rough-and-tumble plays given in the open air on temporary stages in market-places in the Low Countries. In eastern Europe too, travelling bands of entertainers kept alive the tradition of the theatre, though it was not to come to fruition there for many hundreds of years. In western Europe the theatre moved more quickly from one phase to another.

Ill. 43

Ill. 44

44 A farce performed on a portable stage during a sixteenth-century country fair; detail from a painting by Pieter Balten. It shows a husband returning unexpectedly to find his wife hobnobbing with the village priest

CHAPTER THREE

The Theatre of the Italian Renaissance

The medieval religious play reached the peak of its development in the fourteenth century. The fifteenth witnessed its decline, which was hastened by the impact of the Renaissance. This great cultural upheaval began when Constantinople fell to the Turks in 1453, and subsequently the theatre, like all the other arts, underwent a metamorphosis due to its widespread repercussions. By the end of the fifteenth century the enthusiasm of wealthy Italian patrons of drama for plays based on classical models had seriously impaired the standing of the *sacre rappresentazioni*; in Paris the acting of religious plays was forbidden in 1548; in England the Reformation, combined with political expediency, brought them to an end by 1588; and though both the Reformation and the Counter-Reformation had their plays, they were used more for propaganda than for theatrical purposes. Jesuit drama, whose greatest period was yet to come, was scholastic rather than theatrical, and was quick to take advantage of the new classicism, mingling Hercules, tritons and nymphs with saints and martyrs. School drama was very largely educational, and still written in Latin. It was in Spain that the religious play had the longest life. After a late flowering it was forbidden there in 1765.

With the rediscovery of the works of classical drama came the realization that medieval stages, whether for indoor or outdoor performances, were not suitable for their production. Basing themselves on the architectural works of Vitruvius, written *c.* 16–13 BC and first published with illustrations in 1511, theatre architects applied principles of Roman theatre architecture to Italian buildings. With the physical aspects came also the recognition of classical form and restraint, two principles, alien to the sprawling and all-embracing Bible-history, which were to be codified and enforced with greater severity than in classical times. But this was inevitable, as was the fact that it was the late, ornate Hellenistic and Roman theatres that were used as models rather than the simple fifth-century Greek precincts, and that the tragic excesses of Euripides and Seneca, and the more easily accessible comedy of Menander, Plautus and Terence, took precedence over the works of Aeschylus and Aristophanes.

The influence of the new learning spread outwards from Italy in a series of shock-waves, reaching the further shores of western Europe after a time-lag which in some ways lessened the force of the impact and allowed a more thorough assimilation with native culture. Although to Italy must always go the glory of having initiated the Renaissance world, it is sad to have to record that the serious theatre was the least important part of it. Yet two important aspects of theatre – as apart from drama – must be credited to the Italian genius. The first is the form of the new theatre building, with its proscenium arch, and the second is the development of painted scenery. Both these aspects of the theatre are connected with the amazing contemporary development all over Italy in all the plastic and pictorial arts.

Although a careful study of the theatres built under the influence of Vitruvius shows how false in many ways was the Renaissance conception of classical theatre, we must nevertheless take as our point of departure what the new practitioners in theatre building actually designed, because it is from that that our later theatres developed. The key documents in this appraisal are the pictures of *Ills. 45–9* stages in editions of Terence published in 1493 and 1497. One shows a group of scholarly male spectators, possibly a university audience, facing a raised platform between classical pillars with an architectural *Ill. 45* background. Others show a permanent pillared set with actors on *Ill. 47* the platform stage. The four divisions of the background may correspond to the classical stage wall pierced with doors, or to the *frons scaenae* of the Romans, but they also have interesting affinities with the medieval stage, for each doorway represents a 'house' with a name above it. The use of Latin for these superscriptions again indicates an educated and not a popular audience. When we compare *Ills. 33, 36* these two stages with those of the St Apollonia or Valenciennes plays, which may in their turn have undergone some slight influence from the Humanist theatre, what is striking is not so much a radical departure from medieval practice as the imposition of order and

52

45–9 Terence on the Renaissance stage

45 (above) An academic audience waits for a performance, entertained by a musician in front of the stage, labelled 'proscenium'

46 (top right) Calliopius, who appears as the reciter of a Terence play in Ill. 28, speaks the Prologue to the Heauton Timorumenos

47 (centre right) A scene from the Adelphi

48 (bottom right) A scene from the Eunuchus

49 (below) A scene from the Andria. These three woodcuts are almost certainly based on actual performances

50 (*above*) Part of the stage and auditorium of the
Teatro Olimpico, Vicenza, 1580–4, designed
by Palladio and completed by Scamozzi. The
Olimpico, with a façade obviously based on the
frons scaenae of the Roman theatre (*see Ill. 17*)
is the final flowering of Renaissance academic
theatrical architecture

51 (*above right*) Part of the auditorium, seen
from the stage, of the Teatro Farnese, 1618–19,
designed by Aleotti. This theatre, with that of
Scamozzi at Sabbionetta, is a forerunner of
the later European opera-house. Its designer, or
perhaps his pupil Giacomo Torelli (*see Ill. 103*),
provided it with side-wings and backcloth in
place of the fixed archways of earlier theatres
(*see Ill. 50*)

52 (*right*) A design for a stage-set in diagonal
perspective by one of the Bibiena family
(probably Francisco, 1659–1739). It is typical of
the Bibienas' elaborate and grandiose projects

53–5 Three stage settings from Serlio's *Architettura*, 1545: *left to right*, the Comic Scene, the Tragic Scene, and the Satyric Scene. The influence of these three designs, particularly the Satyric Scene, dominated the European theatre for several hundred years, and adaptations of Serlio's trees and cottages formed the setting of innumerable melodramas (*see Ill. 171*)

restraint on the former 'houses' or booths. The forty individual localities of a Mystery cycle are reduced to four, exactly similar. They are usually in a straight line, but could also be grouped into a three-sided arrangement jutting out into the centre of the stage, or set up like a box at one side. There is evidence here of more flexibility than we find later on.

Ills. 48, 49

Ills. 46, 47

When we come to consider Palladio's well-known Teatro Olimpico in Vicenza, with its superb *frons scaenae*, we realize that it is a typical Renaissance theatre in an academic tradition. But so far from being, as was once thought, the starting-point of the modern theatre, it is now considered the final result of a dead-end development, and the future is seen to lie with the development of the Terence stage shown in the 1497 Venice edition of his plays – an open loggia with a small semicircular amphitheatre – by Scamozzi at Sabbionetta and Aleotti in the Teatro Farnese at Parma. It is from these that the horseshoe-shaped auditorium and proscenium-arch stage with its elaborate curtain, typical of later theatre buildings all over the world, were finally evolved. They initiated a style which is only now being ousted from its supremacy by open stages and theatre-in-the-round.

Ill. 50

Ill. 49

Ill. 51

56

The mention of opera-houses reminds us that one outstanding result of the Italian revival in classical style was the great art of opera. A simple play with music, on a mythological or legendary subject, in which the words were paramount was, by the genius of Monteverdi, transmuted into a new art form in which music was all-important. The subject of opera, like that of ballet, is too vast to be dealt with here, though its absence leaves a gap in theatrical history. It would perhaps be more profitable therefore to consider that other adjunct of the opera-house, scenery. This also has its roots in Italy. From there it spread across western Europe until it became a tyranny from which zealous reformers strove to liberate the stage, not always successfully.

Serlio, author of a book on architecture of which the second part, dealing with the theatre, appeared in 1545, was the first scenic artist to publish his designs. His three perspective settings, intended for a theatre in the banqueting-hall of a noble or princely dwelling-house, provided a basic concept which was adhered to by all European scene-designers for the next four hundred years. The sets intended for comedy and tragedy show houses on each side of a street, painted on

Ills. 53, 54

57

56–7 Seventeenth-century masque costumes: (*left*) a 'wild man' or 'monster' by Stefano della Bella; (*right*) a costume representing Prudence, by Henri Gissey

60 (*above*) A *commedia dell'arte* troupe at the Court of Henry of Navarre, *c.* 1578–90, by François Bunel the Younger. A masked *zanni* indicates the horns of cuckoldry above Pantalone's head

61 Pantalone, with Arlecchino and two servants, serenading Donna Lucia, *c.* 1580 ▶

58–9 Two seventeenth-century masque costumes by Lodovico Burnacini, probably for Harlequin though unlike the original character (*see Ills. 61, 65, 70*)

wings and a backcloth. The set for a satyr-play, about which the
Italians knew nothing more than that it was a rustic farce, was a
Ill. 55 country scene of trees with small cottages on each side of the stage.
These three sets form the basis of the work done for the great
Italian entertainments that led to the development of the proscenium
arch, which was originally a pierced wall dividing a room into acting
area and auditorium. They influenced the scenery of the English
masque, the Spanish Court theatre, Molière's theatre in Paris and
nineteenth-century melodrama. They are essentially theatrical, and
even when Serlio's symmetrical scene in perspective, which was
adopted by all his successors, including the Bibienas, was supple-
Ill. 52 mented by the new diagonal perspective perfected by the younger
members of the Bibiena family, Serlio's groupings of buildings and
trees still formed the basis of contrasted town and country scenes.

Of the plays and splendid entertainments given on the Renaissance
Ills. 56–9 stages little remains but the designs for scenery and costume. The
erudite inheritors of the classical tradition wrote with their pens
rather than their heart's blood, and the only ones worthy of mention,
even briefly, are Ariosto, whose comedies are based on Latin
originals, Aretino, less classical and nearer to everyday life, and three
authors remembered for one play each – the cardinal Bibbiena for
Calandria, the statesman Machiavelli for *Mandragola*, and the poet
Tasso for *Aminta*, the first flowering of pastoral comedy. And
perhaps to these may be added the ill-fated Giordano Bruno, whose
Il Candelaio was banned and had what was probably its first stage
performance in Italy in 1905, but whose philosophy, which led him
to be burnt at the stake, may have influenced Shakespeare when
he was writing *Hamlet*.

Even though we may regret the lack of great dramatists, we must
concede that for the beauty of her theatre architecture and her stage
scenery, as well as for the development of opera and ballet – the
latter arising from courtly entertainments in which guests and players
mingled in a final dance – Italy deserves her reputation as the cradle
of the modern theatre. But there was another and even more
important aspect of the Italian theatre which has not yet been touched
on, whose vitality and exuberance may have drained away from

other areas the energies of the theatrically minded, and that is the
commedia dell'arte.   *Ill. 60*

This form of theatre, which appears parallel with the growth of
the serious academic theatre, depended primarily upon the actor and
not the playwright. Its dialogue, from a simple exchange between
two comedians to a full-scale play involving a main and a sub-plot
and a number of actors, was entirely improvised, though a skeleton
plot or scenario was provided to keep the players within bounds.
There were also long stock speeches which, once formulated,
written down and learned by heart, could be adapted to almost any
circumstance. But these were used mainly by the more serious
characters, the young lovers, and also perhaps by the old fathers, the
pedant lawyers and the braggart soldiers. The *zanni*, or comic
servants, whose antics made up the greater and most popular part of   *Ills. 62, 65,*
the entertainment, had less to say, since much of their humour was   *68, 69*
visual, consisting of variations on standard jokes, the *lazzi*, or slighter
comic touches, and the *burle*, longer acts often involving a practical
joke. Both *lazzi* and *burle* afforded the actor great scope for improvisation. By tradition the *zanni* could take the basic situation of the
play in performance as far from its prescribed path as they pleased,
provided they brought it back to a point where the scenario could be
picked up again. That called for a high degree of skill and a quick
wit. But all that we know of the *commedia dell'arte* shows that its
practitioners were unequalled in their profession, combining the
attributes of dancer, singer, acrobat, low comedian, mime and
pantomimist, together with incredible agility of mind and body. A
subtle command of gesture was also essential, as the comic actors
wore masks and so were denied the use of facial expression.   *Ill. 66*

The practice of improvisation was no doubt helped by another
outstanding peculiarity of the *commedia dell'arte*. The company was
made up of actors who always played the same part. This was not
type-casting as we know it today, but the lifelong assumption of a
disguise with which the actor became so identified that he often lost
his own personality in the process, or rather, so merged his own
personality in that of the type he played as to create a distinct
personage. In many cases the actor abandoned his own name for that

62 (*left*) Coviello, who came from Calabria, with a Sicilian friend, playing the guitar and singing, by Bertelli, 1642. He was one of the older men, often the companion of Pantalone, though he sometimes figured as a *zanni* with Pulcinella, whom he somewhat resembled

63 (*right*) Pantalone, by Callot, 1618. He is easily recognizable as Shakespeare's 'lean and slippered pantaloon' in *As You Like It* (II. 7), and later became the foolish old man of the English harlequinade

64 (*far right*) Il Capitano, in Venetian glass from Murano, second half of the sixteenth century

of the character, and so made it even more completely his own. Each *commedia dell'arte* mask – the word is used for the person as well as the thing – belonged to a clearly identifiable group, and it was almost unheard-of for an actor to pass from one group to another, except perhaps in the case of the young lover. If, in later life, he lost his figure or his looks, or developed some useful comic attribute – a paunch or a nutcracker profile – he might abandon his youthful heroics for slapstick and comedy.

The young lovers, who were not particularly interesting in themselves, provided the mainspring of the comedy by their efforts to meet and marry. The heroine usually had a maidservant or confidante called Rosetta or Colombina. Her father, husband, or guardian, who *Ill. 63* tried always to prevent her escape, was a Venetian called Pantalone. He is often depicted as an amorous old man, as Zeus was on the

phlyakes stages. He and his elderly friend, a Bolognese lawyer (Il Dottore) named Graziano, had comic menservants and sometimes shrewish housekeepers. A character somewhat apart from these domestic groups was Il Capitano, a bragging, cowardly soldier, a reincarnation of the *miles gloriosus* of Plautus. He usually assigned to himself some high-sounding title, such as Spezzaferro, Spavento da Vall'Inferno or Matamoros. This last, meaning 'Death to the Moors', was perhaps the most appropriate, since from his earliest appearance, in 1520, Il Capitano seems to have been recognizably Spanish. Perhaps his grotesque appearance, with long crooked nose and enormous moustaches, and his treatment at the hands of the *zanni*, who mock him, trip him up, and prove his valour to be nothing but cowardice, may reflect the feelings of Renaissance Italians towards their hated Spanish tyrants.

Ills. 64, 99

63

Best known of all the stock types are the comic servants. Once the plot had been set in motion, it was their job to keep it going. They were the most numerous and most protean of the *commedia dell'arte* players, and included types from several districts of Italy. It was usual for at least two comic servants to appear in each scenario, one quick-witted, to help the intrigue along, the other a simpleton,
Ill. 65 to act as a foil to his fellow's wit. Among them were Arlecchino,
Ill. 69 Pulcinella, Pedrolino, Scapino, Mezzetino, Scaramuccia, and Brighella. These are all names which in modified forms crop up again later in the history of the theatre.

The origins of the *commedia dell'arte* have been hotly disputed. Efforts have been made to derive it directly from the Greek *phlyakes*, the Roman *atellanae*, or the Imperial mimes. There are similarities to all these in the bawdy, farcical playing and in the emphasis on stock types. Even the name *zanni* has been considered a corruption of the Latin *sannio*, the comic fool of the atellan farce. But the time-lapse is against direct descent from classical times. So is the fact that in the Renaissance theatre written plays appear to have come before the scenario-for-improvisation. In other words, the classical influence, which produced no plays of lasting value, may nevertheless have so worked on the popular mind as to give rise to a form of theatre which had its roots both in its own time and place and in that indestructible mimetic instinct in man, that aptitude of the born comedian for buffoonery, farcical comedy, and improvisation, which resulted in the rustic plays of Greece, of Rome and of Italy, and would even now give rise to similar plays in similar circumstances. All these manifestations of theatrical life resemble each other because they come fundamentally from the same source, and reflect one particular facet of the mind of man. The *commedia dell'arte* may be indebted to earlier forms of farce for some transmitted traditions. But lacking tangible evidence, it is impossible to say that there is direct influence of one form on another.

A good deal is known about the actors and scenarios of the *commedia dell'arte*, and also about the various companies, among them
Ill. 67 the Gelosi, the Confidenti, the Uniti, and the Fedeli. But the story of the actors' migrations from one company to another, and of the

64

65 Arlequin saluting the audience – a characteristic pose – by Dolivar after Le Pautre, seventeenth century. This most famous character of the *commedia dell'arte*, who came from Bergamo, is here portrayed in the transitional stage between Arlecchino and the English Harlequin. He can be seen again in the background, dancing on the far left

continual touring which made up their life, is too complicated to be dealt with in a few lines. From the mid-sixteenth century to the mid-seventeenth troupes of Italian actors travelled all over Europe, in Italy, France and Germany, westward to Spain, eastward to Russia, and even as far north as England. They appeared in London several times in the late sixteenth century, and may have visited the city as early as 1547. Of all the shifting restless population of this colourful and fantastic world a few stand out as individuals. The most famous is perhaps Isabella Andreini, leading lady of the Gelosi, who for the first time made the stereotyped young girl in love (the *innamorata*) the outstanding character. But there were also famous Arlecchinos, Pantalones and Capitanos, whose real names are hidden behind those of their masks.

Ill. 67

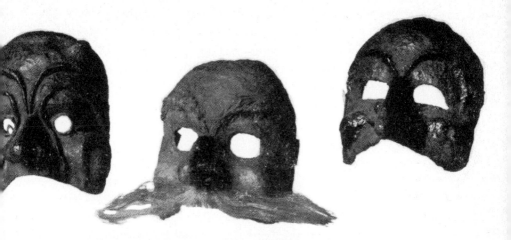

66 (*above*) Three *commedia dell'arte* masks, in leather, probably for *zanni*

67 (*left*) A *commedia dell'arte* troupe, *c.* 1580, probably that of the Gelosi, with Isabella Andreini as the *innamorata* confronting an angry Pantalone

67

There has probably never been so intensely theatrical an institution as the *commedia dell'arte* in its heyday. It owed everything to the actor, very little to drama or literature. It trained its own players, created its own conditions, travelled with its own costumes and properties, sometimes with portable stages like the one seen in *Ill. 68* Callot's engraving of the two *zanni*, Razullo and Cucurucu. A company could consist of as few as five players, or as many as twenty-*Ill. 70* five. The less gifted groups appeared in villages and small towns, the more famous ones in noblemen's halls and kings' palaces. The influence of the *commedia dell'arte* on the theatre of Europe is incalculable. Even when its characters alter out of all recognition, they can be traced back to their originals. From Arlecchino, Colombina and Pantalone come the Harlequin, Columbine and Pantaloon of the nineteenth-century English pantomine. From Pulcinella come the French Polichinelle, the English Punchinello and finally the puppet Punch with his English wife Judy. Pedrolino underwent an even stranger metamorphosis, for he became first the elegant Pierrot of Watteau, then the lovesick, solitary, mournful Pierrot of nineteenth-century Paris, and finally the jolly, gregarious Pierrot of English seaside troupes.

Many other characters from the *commedia dell'arte* are enshrined in the French classical theatre, for as they declined in favour in Italy they started a new career in Paris. French comedies abound in Scapins, *Ills. 151, 162* Scaramouches, and Mezzetins. This part of their history belongs to France, as does their influence on Molière. Shakespeare too must

68 Razullo (with a guitar) and Cucurucu dancing in front of an open-air stage on which a play is being performed, an engraving by Callot, 1621. The stage probably gives a good idea of what the portable *commedia dell'arte* stages were like

Dieſe **Figur** kombt wie hier oben zuſehē heraus,
ū: nach deme ſie auf ihre **Manier** in einen kreiſ
herumb getantzt, ū: nach ſondererkrummer und
ſinckender **pas** gemacht, endigt ſich zu aller zu
ſchauer vergnügen der **Tantz** .

69 Pulcinella dancing, with a smaller Pulcinella below, by Lambranzi, 1716. The
stage is interesting as showing the four pairs of wings and backcloth (perhaps made
up of narrow flats) which originated in the seventeenth century and are still in
use today in opera- and ballet-houses. Pulcinella is the ancestor of the French
Polichinelle and the English Punch

have seen the 'lean and slippered pantaloon', to describe him so accurately.

There is no space to speak of the influence of the Italian comedians. on ballet, though the Peacock Theatre in the Tivoli Gardens in Copenhagen still bears witness to a long-lived tradition. Everywhere in the theatre there are traces of the *commedia dell'arte*. Even the antics of the Keystone Cops, and of Charlie Chaplin, have been attributed to the influence of the *lazzi* and *burle* of the *zanni*. But this may be merely further evidence of the inextinguishable *vis comica* in man's make-up, which has produced all these related forms of farce, and many others which remain uncatalogued. What is certain is that the influence of the *zanni* can be found in all the fools of European farce, whose first names remind us that *zanni* may be a corruption of Giovanni, for they are called John Posset, Jean Potage, *Ill. 135* Jan Bouschet, Hanswurst, Ivanovishka-Douratchok. But it is in their later romantic guise that the descendants of Arlecchino, Pedrolino and their motley companions have captured the imagination of the world. Forgetful of their bawdy, uninhibited early days, their rags transmuted into silken patches and white satin suits, they are no longer Italians or zanies, but the courtly inhabitants of an elegant world painted by such artists as Watteau, Fragonard or *Ill. 151* Lancret.

Inevitably the *commedia dell'arte* declined. The best of it was assimilated by generations of actors all over Europe, but by the end of the seventeenth century it was only a shadow of its former self. Goldoni tried to revive it by providing definitive texts for the actors while retaining the mechanics of their performance. His rival Gozzi, on the other hand, used its masks and methods for improvised comedies which mingled farce with fairy-tale. With him the *commedia dell'arte* had a last blaze of glory before disappearing for ever. Efforts have been made to revive it, but the spirit which animated it has been drawn off into other forms of theatre. Yet the fascination of this important theatrical manifestation remains, and in dealing with it we have been led chronologically far in advance of our time. It was a long-lived product of the Renaissance, to whose repercussions elsewhere we must now return.

70

70 An open-air performance of an Italian comedy, with Arlecchino bowing before ▶ the *innamorata*, Verona, 1772

71

CHAPTER FOUR

The Elizabethan Theatre

Italy, with the *commedia dell'arte*, gave modern Europe its first fully professional actors in organized companies, and also, through the work of Renaissance architects, prepared the way for the development of the indoor theatre with painted scenery and proscenium arch. England was to have the privilege of producing in Shakespeare the first modern playwright fit to stand comparison with the masters of Greek drama. He began writing while the Elizabethan theatre was still in its infancy, but the influences which moulded him, and shaped his work, are to be found as much in his own country as on the Continent.

While the sixteenth-century holiday-crowds were still enjoying performances of Bible-histories on pageant-wagons, and of Morality plays like *Hickscorner*, with its lusty personification of Freewill and Imagination, or *Nice Wanton*, on the theme of 'spare the rod and spoil the child', the first English Renaissance comedy, *Ralph Roister Doister*, was being written by a schoolmaster, Nicholas Udall, for performance by his pupils. A decade later, in 1562, a Renaissance tragedy, *Gorboduc*, based on Seneca, was prepared by two scholars of the Inner Temple, Thomas Norton and Thomas Sackville, for performance by their fellow-students in the presence of Queen Elizabeth I. These were amateur productions for an educated audience. More acceptable to a popular audience were the Interludes, one-act comedies which show a mingling of native farce with classical allusions. For instance, in *The Play of the Weather*, by John Heywood, a number of people are shown praying to Jove for weather suitable to their own needs, which conflict with those of the other characters. Heywood's Interludes, and those of Rastell and Redford, were acted by groups of players maintained as part of their household by rich men and the nobility, and were probably
Ill. 71   given in a setting of houses on each side of a street which owed

72

something to Renaissance Italy. It was from these groups of Interlude players that the first professional English actors finally emerged. They added to their repertory such popular tragi-comedies as Preston's *Cambyses* and the long chronicle-plays which used the episodic method of the Bible-history for stories from English history, and acted them, and many others now lost, on platform stages set up in innyards, which formed excellent temporary theatres. But before the theatre could develop freely, England, like Italy, needed theatre buildings, with conditions of stability in which actor and dramatist alike could relax and feel at home.

The first permanent theatre in London was built, appropriately enough, by a carpenter, James Burbage, who was also a part-time *Ill. 74* actor, obviously a man born for the theatre. Of his two sons, the younger, Richard, was the first leading English actor, the creator of *Ill. 73* Hamlet, Lear, Othello, and Richard III, while the elder, Cuthbert, acted as his brother's manager.

The building which the elder Burbage erected in 1576 was known simply as 'The Theatre'. It was an enclosed structure of wood, which, *Ill. 74* because of opposition from the Lord Mayor of London to the very

71 A scene from the *Interlude of the Four Cardinal Virtues*, in a woodcut of *c.* 1547

73

idea of a theatre, was built outside the city boundary, in Finsbury Fields. Very little is known about it, or about the other Elizabethan theatres which sprang up as soon as Burbage's venture was seen to be successful. They were, roughly in chronological order, the Curtain, *Ills. 75, 78* the Rose, the Swan, the Globe, the Fortune, and the Hope. Of these the Rose, the Fortune, and the Hope belonged to Philip Henslowe, a shrewd business man who leased his theatres to various companies, and also paid the bills for playscripts, costumes and properties while they were in occupation. In return he received a large share of the daily takings. His stepdaughter Joan married the other outstanding *Ill. 72* actor of the period, Richard Burbage's only rival, Edward Alleyn, who inherited his father-in-law's property and papers. Among the latter was his diary, an invaluable source of information on the theatre of his time. This is now in Dulwich College, which was founded by Alleyn.

The most famous Elizabethan theatre, round which controversy constantly rages, is the Globe, built by James Burbage's sons on London's South Bank in 1599 with timber from 'The Theatre'. It was here that most of Shakespeare's plays were produced, and it was after a performance of his *Henry VIII* in 1612 that the theatre was destroyed by fire. It was rebuilt the following year and remained in *Ill. 78* use until 1644, when it was demolished.

None of the Elizabethan theatres survived, and all the information about them comes from a few builder's specifications, some scattered descriptions in letters and essays, and a very few illustrations, most of them of a later date. The only one which is known to be con- temporary is a copy of a drawing of the Swan Theatre, made by a *Ill. 75* Dutchman, Johannes de Witt, during a visit to London in about 1596. It is not very clear, but it does seem to show the main features of an Elizabethan unroofed public playhouse. These were the raised platform-stage, sometimes railed, with an open space for standing spectators on three sides, and round that two or three galleries furnished with benches or stools. This roughly represents the set-up of the innyard. Behind the platform-stage was a wall, with doors or curtained doorways which gave access backstage. This wall supported a gallery for musicians or actors, surmounted by a tower housing

74

72–3 The two best-known Elizabethan actors, (*left*) Edward Alleyn, 1566–1626, (*right*) Richard Burbage, *c.* 1567–1619, from portraits in the Dulwich College Picture Gallery

machinery. From this tower a trumpet-call announced the opening of the play, and a flag was flown during the performance, which usually took place in the early afternoon. Over the stage itself was a canopy, known as the 'heavens'. It was supported on columns, and the ceiling was painted blue, with golden stars. If the auditorium shows the influence of the innyard, the stage and its surroundings seem to owe more to the architectural background of the Continental theatre, with a marked classical derivation. There is also some suggestion of the triumphal arches and temporary monuments set up at fixed points in the city for royal visits and processions of all kinds. The only reminders of the Bible-history stage are the unlocalized *platea* or platform-stage (which in the absence of changeable scenery could represent any place needed for the action of the play), the trapdoors in the stage, and the machinery in the tower.

Ill. 76
Ill. 77

75

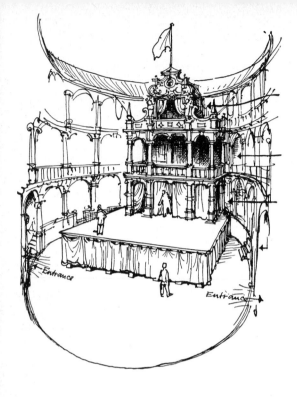

porticus

orchestra

mimorum ædes

proscænium

planities siue arena

74 (*above left*) A reconstruction of James Burbage's theatre, known as 'The Theatre', built in 1576

75 (*above centre*) A copy of Johannes de Witt's drawing of the Swan Theatre of *c.* 1596 – the only contemporary picture of an Elizabethan theatre interior in existence

76–7 (*bottom left and centre*) The design of Continental ceremonial stages such as this Rederijkers stage, Antwerp, 1561, influenced British triumphal arches like those for James I's Coronation in 1603 (*centre*, the arch near the Royal Exchange, in Cornhill), and by inference, the London stages which so much resembled them (cf. *Ill. 74*)

78 (*above*) The exterior of the second Globe Theatre, 1616

79 (*left*) The platform stage used for William Alabaster's *Roxana*, shown in a woodcut of 1632

One of the features of the Elizabethan theatre which has caused acute controversy is the so-called 'inner stage'. This is believed to have been either a room built out behind the central opening, or part of the corridor running behind the stage wall. In either case it could be revealed by the drawing of a curtain. But some theatre historians think there never was such an inner stage. There is no sign *Ill. 75* of it in de Witt's drawing, which shows only two side doors. There is, however, no reason to suppose that all Elizabethan theatre buildings were exactly alike. And if the inner stage did not exist something like it must have been erected at the back of the main stage for such scenes as that in *The Tempest*, where Miranda and Ferdinand are 'discovered' playing chess. As we shall see later, the evidence of the *Ill. 92* Spanish stage speaks strongly in favour of the inner stage, as does perhaps the Terence-stage also.

In his description of the Swan, de Witt said the interior had a flint-and-mortar wall between wooden columns 'painted in exact imitation of marble'. The Elizabethans were excellent architects and great lovers of decorative work, and there is no reason to suppose that their theatres were less lavish than their other public buildings. The marble pillars may have been part of a scheme of gold and red and blue to which the bright costumes of the actors, the stage hangings, and the banners and pageantry of the royal or military processions in the play all added their quota of gaiety. The greater part of the actors' wardrobes was made up of discarded robes given to them by wealthy patrons. These would have seemed very splendid to the audience, which included persons from every walk of life, men and women, young and old. They would also have been contemporary in style, whatever the period of the play, but with some conventional details for certain characters, such as a breastplate and kilt for a Roman soldier, a turban for a Turk, long robes for other Orientals, and a gaberdine for a Jew. The only drawing known of Elizabethan actors *Ill. 81* in stage costume, showing a group from *Titus Andronicus* in 1595, is a good example of the mixing of contemporary and conventional dress.

The companies which appeared in the Elizabethan theatres were all under the patronage of some noble person, since masterless men,

78

80 William Shakespeare (1564–1616), the so-called 'Chandos' portrait ▶

even actors, were still classed officially as 'rogues and vagabonds'. Burbage and Shakespeare belonged to the Lord Chamberlain's Men, Alleyn to the Admiral's. But the rules governing each company varied, particularly as the actors gained in confidence and stability. In Shakespeare's company the actors owned their own playhouse, prompt-books, costumes and properties, and each held shares in the undertaking which entitled him to a fixed part of the profits. This was probably something like the way in which the *commedia dell'arte* companies had been organized, except that they had no permanent theatre buildings. Alleyn's company, however, paid rent to Henslowe and received salaries from him.

As in Greece, there were no women on the Elizabethan stage. Boys, specially selected for their slight, graceful build and light

81 (*above*) Characters in *Titus Andronicus*, from a manuscript by Henry Peachum, 1595, with Aaron as a blackamoor

82 (*right*) Richard Tarleton, c. 1590. He was described as short, thick-set, slightly hump-backed, with a squint and a comically flattened nose

83 (*far right*) William Kempe dancing, woodcut of 1600 from his own account of his morris-dance from London to Norwich, undertaken for a wager. Kempe succeeded Tarleton in the affections of the public

voices, were apprenticed to older actors and trained to play such parts as Juliet, Rosalind, Viola and Portia. The comedians of the troupe played the older women like Juliet's Nurse or Mistress Quickly. As in Italy, all the actors had to be dancers and singers, sometimes instrumentalists, for music played a large part in the plays, and in the jigs which followed them. These jigs, which were dances with sung dialogue, were immensely popular with Elizabethan audiences, and the actor William Kempe was particularly admired for *Ill. 83* his performances in them. The clowns and fools who appear in so many Elizabethan plays may, like the *zanni* of the *commedia dell'arte*, had been in the habit of extemporizing, and it is thought that Shakespeare, when he made Hamlet say to the players, 'Let those that play your fools speak no more than is set down for them', had in mind the comedian Richard Tarleton, who was famous for his *Ill. 82* improvisations. It is even possible that some of the more obscure jokes in Shakespeare's plays may be the result of impromptu remarks which became incorporated into the written script. As plays were valuable properties, they were kept in manuscript as long as possible and jealously guarded by the company which owned them. Even Shakespeare's plays were not gathered together for publication until after his death. Many by lesser authors have completely disappeared, and are known only by their titles.

It was indeed fortunate that Shakespeare's plays were printed, for none of his manuscripts survived, and in spite of his world-wide *Ill. 80* reputation little is known about him. Born perhaps in Stratford-upon-Avon, in one of the midland counties of England, Warwickshire, he married there at eighteen, but soon after went to London, where he became first an actor and then a playwright and a shareholder in the Globe Theatre. Having prospered in his theatrical affairs, he bought himself a pleasant house in Stratford and retired there to die in 1616, leaving two daughters married to Stratford citizens. His only son died at the age of eleven. That is practically all we know for certain about Shakespeare's life. The rest must be looked for in his plays, which are amazingly varied in style and scope, ranging from tragedy to comedy with excursions into history, tragi-comedy, romantic tragedy, and pastoral. Very often the plays escape classification, for Shakespeare was a universal genius, and in his work comedy and tragedy are as closely interwoven as they are in the lives of all human beings. Like quicksilver, Shakespeare escapes when one tries to contain him within the definitions which serve well enough for lesser writers. Most of his plays were written for the public stage, and careful study of them has revealed much information about the structure and use of the Elizabethan stage, particularly at the Globe Theatre.

In his own day Shakespeare was not as highly esteemed as he is now. His contemporaries, with the exception of Ben Jonson, looked down on him as a hack-writer who was not, like most other dramatists of the period, a university man. We owe the first reference to Shakespeare as a dramatist – a disparaging one – to one of the so-called 'university wits', Robert Greene, who called him (in *A Groatsworth of Wit bought with a Million of Repentance*) 'an upstart crow . . . and in his opinion the only Shake-scene in the country'. Greene's malice may have been prompted by jealousy, for he was not as successful as Shakespeare, nor indeed as his other university friends. Among them was Thomas Kyd, author of a revenge play, *The Spanish Tragedy*, and perhaps of an early version of *Hamlet*, both of which may have influenced Shakespeare when he came to write his finest work.

It was Kyd's friend Christopher Marlowe, a Cambridge man, born in the same year as Shakespeare but active in the theatre before him, who opened a new era in English dramatic history with his plays, which included a dramatized version of the legend of Doctor Faustus. An illustration in a printed copy of this shows Mephistopheles, like Satan in the Bible-histories, dressed in a black suit, masked, appearing through a trapdoor in the stage.

Ill. 84

Marlowe, who was a poet as well as a playwright, abandoned the short jigging rhymed verse in which earlier plays had been written, and by his superb manipulation of the iambic pentameter prepared the way for Shakespeare's poetic drama. He might even have equalled Shakespeare in reputation had he not been stabbed to death in a tavern brawl shortly before his thirtieth birthday.

A very different sort of man from either Marlowe or Shakespeare was Ben Jonson. After receiving a good education at Westminster, he was deprived of a university education by the action of his stepfather, who took him away from school and apprenticed him to his own trade of brick-laying. Unlike Shakespeare, Jonson was always conscious of his lack of university status, and allowed it to embitter him. Frustrated, quarrelsome, he was often in trouble with the authorities, and several times in prison. But nothing stopped him from speaking and writing as he thought fit. He was perhaps more strongly influenced by the Renaissance than any other English

84 A scene from Marlowe's *Doctor Faustus* (c. 1589), a woodcut of 1636

dramatist. Marlowe, Kyd and Shakespeare all retained in their work something of the earlier forms of English drama. Jonson, steeped in the classical authors, brought considerable erudition to the composition of his plays, and imposed on them the five-act form advocated by Horace. In this he was imitated by the first editors of Shakespeare, the actors Heminge and Condell, who cut up into arbitrary sections what should be a continuous free-flowing whole.

Jonson's tragedies are frigid and forgotten, but his satiric comedies, in the first of which, *Everyman in His Humour*, Shakespeare played Knowell, had a lasting influence on the development of English comedy, and the best of them continue to be popular on the stage.

All the authors mentioned so far wrote mainly for open-air public *Ills. 75, 78* theatres like the Swan and the Globe. But at the turn of the century many plays were written for the indoor or private theatres set up in Blackfriars and elsewhere. These had the advantage of being usable in bad weather, or even in the winter, being roofed and lit by candles. The audience, less numerous but better educated, demanded a more subtle style in plot and dialogue and more elaborate equipment. In *Ill. 85* appearance the second Blackfriars Theatre, built, like the first, in the ruins of the old monastery, was more like the Renaissance theatres of Italy than were the earlier Elizabethan theatres. It was rectangular, with a stage across one of the shorter sides and the audience seated in front of it on benches. Although it retained from the public theatre the back wall with doors and a gallery above, it seems to have had a simultaneous setting like that shown in the *Ills. 45–9* Renaissance Terence-stages, which were still being used in France. There was also, in later years, painted scenery, which came from *Ill. 88* Italy by way of the masques performed at Court.

The Blackfriars Theatre was used mainly by adult companies, but it was leased sometimes to the boy-actors drawn from the choir-schools of St Paul's and the Chapel Royal, for whom Ben Jonson wrote some excellent comedies on classical themes. They had earlier appeared with great success in a smaller theatre near by, when their chief playwright had been John Lyly, better known as the author of the novel *Euphues*. The audience no doubt delighted in the grace and artificiality of his dialogue, and his sly references to contem-

84

85 A reconstruction of the second Blackfriars Theatre, built by James Burbage in
1597. This theatre was for many years the winter home of the King's Men, the
company to which Shakespeare belonged, and was also leased to the children of
the Chapel Royal and St Paul's, who appeared there in a number of plays of which
the most important were those by Ben Jonson, *Cynthia's Revels* and *The Poetaster*.
There is no evidence for the use of footlights

porary scandals may have had an added piquancy coming from the lips of young boys. One of Lyly's plays, at least, was first performed at Court, for although England never had a Court theatre in the sense in which it was later understood on the Continent, players formed part of the royal household from the earliest times, and entertainments were regularly given at Court on feast-days. The mummings and disguisings devised for royal occasions may not have been as splendid as those of Italy and France, but they existed. Professional actors too were pressed into service, and Shakespeare's *Twelfth Night* may have been seen at Court before it appeared on the public stage. This would have involved a certain amount of reorganization, for the play would have been given in a hall adapted for the purpose, with a few light canvas structures representing bowers, rocks, or rooms arranged in advance for the actors' use, and not on a bare platform-stage, as at the Globe.

88 *(right)* Inigo Jones' Tragic Scene. There is no proof that the design was ever ▶ used, but it was evidently meant for a private playhouse in which a Palladian arch could be combined with scenic devices

86–7 *(below)* Two costume designs by Inigo Jones: left, Penthesilea, from *The Mask of Queens*, 1609; right, Oberon, from *Oberon, the Fairy Prince*, 1611

It was, however, the Court masques of the early seventeenth century that were important in the development of the English theatre, particularly those produced by Inigo Jones from 1605 to 1613, for several of which Ben Jonson wrote the words. Jones, who was an artist and an architect, travelled widely in Italy and came into close contact with scenic artists there. From them he took the idea of a painted backcloth with side wings which he used in the productions staged at Whitehall. It is interesting to see how closely his Tragic Scene corresponds to that of Serlio. Jones' designs for *Ills. 54, 88* scenery and costumes, many of which have been preserved, are elaborately ornate, and could not have been used in the public *Ills. 86, 87* theatres of the time. They demanded not only the enclosed conditions of a great hall or private theatre, but also some form of proscenium arch. They also tended to distract attention from the dialogue, which caused Jonson to give up writing masques, not wishing, as he said, to

89 A platform-stage with footlights (found for the first time on an English stage) and a curtained booth at the back, from the frontispiece to Francis Kirkman's *The Wits*; or, *Sport upon Sport*, published in 1673

compete with the carpenter and scene-painter. The use of scenery had already spread from the Court to Blackfriars by 1637, and might, in some modified form, have reached the public playhouses had it not been for the Civil War, which put an end to theatre-going.

After the age of Shakespeare the English theatre, perhaps inevitably, suffered a decline. There were good actors, but none as good as Burbage and Alleyn; good playwrights, but none as good as Shakespeare and Jonson. There were no innovations in public-theatre design or production to revive interest in the art of the theatre. The buildings were getting shabby. The last one, the Fortune, was built in 1600. The Hope, which opened in 1613, was only the old Bear Garden, converted for use as a playhouse. The

90 Itinerant actors, and a platform-stage set up in a market-place, *c.* 1651–76. Although this may depict conditions in France in the mid-seventeenth century, its details are probably valid for any European troupe of itinerant actors

private theatres attracted a limited audience, the Court plays were designed for the personal entourage of the monarch. In such plays as survive we can see a definite change in style. In the hands of the playwrights Beaumont and Fletcher, who began their collaboration in 1608, high tragedy and low comedy, as understood by Shakespeare, became entangled with romance, or were discarded altogether in favour of pastorals like *The Faithful Shepherdess*. The satiric humour of Jonson lost its bite and degenerated into the mild ridicule of the citizen and his wife in *The Knight of the Burning Pestle*. Plays like these were intended for the amusement of a sophisticated audience far removed from the groundlings of the Globe who had enjoyed the robust bawdry of Shakespeare's clowns and the savagery

89

of Jonson's *Volpone*. The only outstanding talent to emerge before civil war broke out in 1642 was that of John Webster, whose *White Devil* and *Duchess of Malfi* were strong Italian Renaissance tragedies of political intrigue written in splendidly passionate poetic dialogue and staged with extreme realism.

When war was finally declared the theatre was the first casualty. The theatres were closed and acting forbidden, and the actors dispersed to join the army or find some other means of livelihood. The Puritan so graphically portrayed by Ben Jonson in *Bartholomew Fair* had triumphed, and London was to remain officially without a theatre until 1660, though surreptitious performances of short plays were sometimes given. Some of these were published later in *The*
Ill. 89 *Wits*, whose frontispiece shows actors on a stage similar to that of the Globe, but with footlights, a startling innovation.

English theatrical tradition took a long time to recover from the shock of eighteen years without a theatre. People lost the habit of playgoing, the older generation of actors vanished almost without trace, and when the theatre resumed its activities in 1660 it had none of that strong sense of continuity which distinguishes, for example, the French theatre, though France, and through France Spain, were to have a great influence on the new English scene.

CHAPTER FIVE

The Golden Age of Spain and France

Although the development of the English and the Spanish theatres runs parallel, and their theatre buildings show many similarities, there seems to have been little or no contact between them, probably as a result of the political situation. English acrobats are mentioned as touring in Spain only a few years after the opening of The Theatre in London in 1576, and they may have taken back news of Madrid's new buildings to Burbage and Henslowe. But the plays of Spain's Golden Age seem to have been as unknown to English dramatists as theirs were to the Spaniards. It was not until the Restoration that Spanish dramatic literature, through the intermediary of France, made any impact upon England.

The early history of the Spanish theatre, with the development of religious plays in the vernacular, secular farces from popular sources, and Renaissance comedies played against a street scene reminiscent of Serlio's perspective design, resembles that of Italy and other European countries. It was at first closely bound up with the emergent theatre of Portugal, and indeed one of the first playwrights, Gil Vicente, was Portuguese. In his plays, and in those of his contemporaries, two themes which were to be important later on – the pastoral and the romantic – are already apparent. It was perhaps to satirize the chivalric and romantic tendency of the time that there appeared in 1499 *La Celestina*, a prose work in dramatic form which though not intended for the stage (it is in twenty-one acts) was probably read aloud, as the plays of Terence and Seneca were, and had a great influence on the work of later playwrights through its racy and realistic dialogue.

One of the first 'men of the theatre' in Spain, in the modern sense, was Lope de Rueda, an actor-manager and author of a number of short farces or *pasos* designed to amuse the audience between the acts of the more serious plays in which he toured with his company,

91 Lope de Vega (1562–1635), Spain's first important playwright, and virtually the founder of the Spanish theatre, in an engraving by M. S. Larmona

92 (*below*) The Corral del Príncipe, Madrid; a seventeenth-century reconstruction by Juan Comba. The resemblance to the Elizabethan 'innyard' auditorium is striking (*see Ills. 74, 75*). A point to be noticed is the indication of an inner stage (see p. 78)

93 (*below right*) A masked ball in the Teatro del Príncipe, Madrid, 1766, a painting by L. Paret. In comparison with *Ill. 92*, this shows the marked influence on Spanish theatre architecture of the typical Italian opera-house

playing in noblemen's halls and in the 'yards' or *corrales* between buildings. These, like the innyards of England, provided ready-made playing-places, and when the first professional theatres were built they incorporated several features of the *corral*. The audience stood in the courtyard (*patio*) or sat in the surrounding galleries and boxes. There was a special gallery for women, and behind the stage, which projected out into the auditorium, was a balcony reached by a flight of steps. The back wall had doors and windows, and there was definitely an inner stage, like the much-disputed inner stage of the Elizabethan theatre, which could be revealed by drawing back a curtain. There were also trapdoors in the stage floor and machinery for lowering cloud-borders, thrones or divine apparitions from above. The whole thing, in fact, was remarkably like the theatres of London. Several of these theatres were built in different parts of Spain, but the two most important were the Corral de la Cruz (1579) and the Corral del Príncipe (1582), both in Madrid. When, many years later, the Madrid theatres were rebuilt in the Italian fashion, the most important retained an echo of earlier days in its name, the Teatro del Príncipe.

Ill. 92

Ills. 74, 75

Ill. 93

The professional actor in Spain was much influenced by the visits of the *commedia dell'arte* companies, particularly that led by Ganassa. Under Italian influence structural changes were introduced into the design of the stage to facilitate the production of plays, and a high standard of acting was set. Among the authors, many of them directly influenced by classical dramatists, particularly Seneca, or by contemporary Italian writers, whose works were performed in these theatres, was Cervantes. Besides the immortal *Don Quixote* he wrote ten plays and a number of short interludes or *entremeses* given between the acts of his full-length plays, of which the best was his one tragedy, *Numancia*. At this time plays in Spain were bought outright from the dramatist by the manager of the company which wished to perform them. The actors made yearly contracts with the managers, drawing a fixed salary, in the style of Henslowe's companies in London rather than in that of Shakespeare's Globe.

Ill. 91 The theatre in Spain was firmly established by the brilliance and fecundity of Lope de Vega, the first outstanding Spanish playwright. He is credited with having written twelve hundred plays, of which only about seven hundred and fifty survive. Such an enormous output argues not only a great facility in composition, but an insatiable demand on the part of the audience for new works, a demand which Lope de Vega, known in his own days as 'a monster of nature', was quite capable of satisfying. His plays, which are written in free-flowing verse, deal with every possible subject – religious, historical, pastoral and social – and portray an idealized Christian, indeed Catholic, society firmly divided into three estates, kings, nobles, and commons (usually peasants). The king, with the help of his nobles, rules; the commons are ruled. But rulers have duties as well as rights, the peasants have rights as well as duties. This is the background of such a play as *Fuenteovejuna* (*The Sheepfold*), which depicts not only the revolt of the villagers against a brutal overlord (thus qualifying, in some quarters, as the first Communist play of class warfare) but also the revolt of the overlord against the king. The nobleman thus fails in his duty to his underlings as well as to his superior, and must be removed from office before harmony can be restored.

94

A fruitful source of comedy in the works of Lope de Vega is the contrast between the wicked town (in which most of his middle-class audience lived) and the virtuous countryside. Indeed, as with Ben Jonson, the censuring of the faults of urban society was a rich source of satiric drama, particularly in the works of Lope de Vega's younger contemporary, Juan Ruíz de Alarcón, who was born in Mexico and taken to Spain when very young. He was a cripple, and the ridicule attracted by his physical deformity may perhaps explain and excuse the bitterness apparent in his work and his constant hostility to other writers, particularly Lope de Vega. Though his plays are ingenious and well constructed, they were less popular in Spain than in France. His sobriety and elegance made him more accessible as a model for French writers than the exuberant Lope de Vega.

When even Lope de Vega's abundant energy began to flag, he was succeeded as Spain's chief playwright by Pedro Calderón de la Barca, of whose plays more than two hundred survive. The early ones are comedies of intrigue – variations on the theme of honour – and moral and social comedies written for the public theatres. The best known of them is probably *El alcalde de Zalamea*, a study of vice and virtue in a setting which recalls Lope de Vega's vision of the orderly class-conscious society of contemporary Spain. For the Court Theatre at the palace of Buen Retiro, the Coliseo, which opened in 1640, Calderón prepared mythological spectacles of great splendour, intended to make full use of the latest Italian devices in the way of perspective scenery and concealed lighting with which it was equipped. It is interesting to see, in the designs for one of his Court productions, the obvious use of wings and backcloths, which make the illustrations more realistic than is usual in theatre designs of the time. The success of these Court spectacles contributed not a *Ill. 95* little to the decline of the commercial theatre, after Calderón's death, in favour of imported Italian opera.

Even in his youth Calderón, who became a priest in 1651, had written a number of religious plays, *autos sacramentales*, and in later life he wrote nothing else. Professor A. A. Parker, in his study of Calderón's religious works, says of him that 'he is a theological poet

94 Design for a Court Theatre in Spain, attributed to F. Ricci, *c.* 1680, and showing the influence of the Spanish Baroque architects, the Churrigueras, who flourished from 1680 onwards

and dramatist in a deep and legitimate sense, and as such his achievement is not only valuable, but unique'. The best known of his *autos* is *El gran teatro del mundo*, on the theme of 'all the world's a stage', with each man playing throughout his life the part allotted to him by God at birth. Although Calderón lacked Lope de Vega's facility and Alarcón's mordant satire, he was a subtle writer and a most excellent craftsman, and his plays were destined to exert an important influence on the European theatre, an influence which penetrated even to England.

One other contemporary of Lope de Vega whose work was to reappear frequently in European dramatic literature was Tirso de

95 A stage setting for one of Calderón's plays, 1690, with side-wings and backcloth in the Italian style. In the background is a ship which is about to be wrecked,
in the foreground are Cupid, Aeolus, a chorus of sea nymphs, Neptune and Mars

Molina, a writer of deep psychological intensity, at his best in the
portrayal of women, and the author of the first play on the legendary
story of Don Juan.

If the form of the early Spanish stage resembled that of England,
its plays were very different, and the most difficult for an English
audience to appreciate are those that turn on the famous *pundonor*, or
point of honour. In them action takes precedence over character, and
the moral theme is simplified to the point of abstraction. There are
no half-tones. A bad action is recognized as such even by its perpe-
trator. There are no mitigating circumstances, and the evildoer must
be punished, even if the punishment recoils on an innocent head.

It was this particular aspect of the Spanish theatre – perhaps the most characteristic, if not necessarily the most popular or prolific – that was to influence France so strongly that the modern French
Ill. 101 theatre dates its inception from *Le Cid*, a play on the early life of Spain's national hero written by Pierre Corneille, and produced in 1637. Its plot exemplifies perfectly the Spanish *pundonor*, for it shows a son avenging an insult to his aged father by killing the father of his own fiancée. Up to 1637 the French theatre had followed much the same path as the theatre elsewhere. But in 1548 the Confraternity of the Passion, which held the monopoly of acting in Paris, was forbidden to appear in the debased and secularized religious plays which formed its traditional repertory. This left the commercial theatre free to develop in its own way. The process was delayed by the ravages of civil war, and the sixteenth century, which saw the firm establishment of the professional theatre in England and Spain, was still a period of experiment and confusion. But the influence of the
Ill. 43 Renaissance finally prevailed over the indigenous farces and *soties*, as

98 (*right*) French actors at the Hôtel de Bourgogne, Paris, *c*. 1630. On-stage are ▶ Turlupin, Gaultier-Garguille and Gros-Guillaume (*see also Ills. 99, 100*) interestingly reminiscent of Arlecchino, Pantalone and Pedrolino (or Pulcinella)

96 (*below*) Italian *commedia dell'arte* players in France, from the *Recueil Fossard*, *c*. 1577. In spite of the French names given to the characters, the central figure is obviously Pantalone and the woman Franceschina

97 A simultaneous setting by the designer Mahelot, with a wood, a street and a house, for Alexandre Hardy's *Cornélie*, performed at the Hôtel de Bourgogne, Paris, between 1625 and 1635

well as over the Bible-histories, and the new drama was established with plays on classical themes by scholars of the new learning. Unlike English dramatists, who mingled grave and gay in equal proportions, French writers, following what they believed to be the classical model, made a sharp distinction between the two, a distinction which was to be upheld and indeed intensified by the later dramatists of the seventeenth century. It faltered somewhat in the hands of the first professional French playwright, Alexandre Hardy, however. His numerous tragi-comedies were written for a troupe of actors and actresses – the French stage was never an all-male preserve but had young and beautiful leading ladies from the very first – who can fairly be considered the first fully-professional French players to appear in Paris, though they had been preceded there by some

Ill. 96   *commedia dell'arte* troupes. Under Valleran-Lecomte they established themselves in the old theatre of the Hôtel de Bourgogne leased to

Ill. 98   them by the Confraternity of the Passion. This was a long narrow room – Paris never had unroofed theatres like those of London and Madrid – with a platform-stage at one end. In front of it was a pit for standing spectators only, extending back to tiers of rising benches, with boxes at the side. Both stage and auditorium were lit by candles, and all the plays were presented in the old-fashioned simultaneous

Ill. 97   setting which can be seen in the designs by Mahelot, stage-designer for Valleran-Lecomte's company. These show that Italian scene design had not yet ousted the older forms. The plays themselves were to some extent exercises in rhetoric, since each actor advanced to the edge of the stage to declaim his lines, and then retired to make way for his successor.

It was not long before Paris had several theatres, all planned after the same model, where a curious mixture of plays can be noted, remnants of the old Mysteries and Moralities surviving side by side with new plays written under classical or Italian influence. Most of them were pastorals or tragi-comedies; comedy in the true sense seems not to have been popular. Farces, however, were still much in favour, and the most famous actors of the day were the farce-players

Ills. 98–100   Turlupin, Gaultier-Garguille and Gros-Guillaume. But there were a number of good serious actors ready to interpret the plays of France's

100

100 A composite painting, *c.* 1670, in which French actors of the 1630s, some of ▶ them derived from characters of the *commedia dell'arte*, mingle with players of thirty years later, among them Molière and Poisson

Capitaine fracasse · Turlupin · Gros Guillaume · Gaultier Garguille

99 The chief comedians, right, of the Hôtel de Bourgogne, *c.* 1630. There are hints of the *commedia dell'arte* masks in these three, but they have evolved into truly French comic figures, whereas the swaggering Capitano of earlier times has now dwindled, left, into Le Capitaine Fracasse, a *figurant* (or super)

delef. Poisson. Turlupin. *Le Capitan Matamore.* Arlequin. Guillot Gorju. Gros Guillaume. LeDottor Grazian Balourd. Gaultier Garguille polichinelle. Pantalon. Philippin. Scaramouche. Briquelle.

outstanding dramatists when they finally appeared. Montdory and Mlle de Villiers, with an experienced company, had no hesitation in

Ill. 101 tackling *Le Cid* when it was produced at their theatre in the Marais.

The form of Elizabethan drama flowered naturally in the hands of dramatists who were also, for the most part, actors. The form of French tragedy was imposed from without, with the codifying of the three unities of time, place and action, derived by literary critics from the works of Aristotle. They were first adhered to in the pastoral, which became popular after the appearance of a translation of Tasso's *Aminta*. The history of the battle for the unities belongs to the domain of literature rather than of the theatre. The restrictions they imposed, which would have been intolerable to English writers, suited the French love of order and seemliness, and those plays in which the writers adhered to the unities seem to have been more successful with the public than those which did not. The necessity for setting the action within a confined space – a courtyard or a room in a palace – and of resolving the conflict within a limited time, usually twenty-four hours, certainly heightened the tension and made an impact upon the spectator.

Corneille, to whom goes the honour of inaugurating France's greatest dramatic era, was a native of Rouen, where his first play, a comedy, was performed by a strolling company which had come to present some of Hardy's plays in the town. He had moved to Paris, written several more plays, and been chosen by Richelieu to fabricate dramatic literature to order – a servitude to which he was temperamentally unsuited – when his attention was drawn to *Las Mocedades del Cid*, a chronicle-play on the exploits of the great Spanish hero by Castro y Bellvís, a contemporary of Lope de Vega. On this he based

Ill. 101 his tragi-comedy *Le Cid*, which, though accused of violating the precious unities and therefore not received with universal acclaim by the critics, nevertheless established him as the leading playwright of France. He proceeded to consolidate his position with a series of excellent tragedies on classical subjects. He also dipped into Spanish

Ill. 102 drama again and produced a good comedy, *Le Menteur*, based on Alarcón's play about a man who lies so readily that when he speaks the truth he is not believed.

101–2 Engravings from a 1764 edition of Corneille's plays: (*left*) *Le Cid*, 1637; (*right*) *Le Menteur*, 1643

103 A setting by Giacomo Torelli for Corneille's spectacle-play *Andromède*, 1649

Corneille continued to write until about ten years before his death, and among his works is a charming classical spectacle *Andromède*, written to show off the Italian scenery and machinery imported into *Ill. 103* France by the great Torelli. In his later years he found himself engaged in rivalry with the young Jean Racine, a playwright destined to carry on and perfect the form of tragedy initiated by Corneille. Racine's best play, *Phèdre*, shows all his gifts to perfection. The lyric beauty of its dialogue, the subtlety of its psychology, the tension of its tightly wound plot make it a masterpiece of dramatic literature. Its leading character, which is a test-piece for all actresses *Ill. 104* aspiring to greatness, was first played by Mlle Champmeslé, who was also the interpreter of many of Racine's other heroines, among *Ill. 106* them Bérénice in the tragedy of that name, and for a time his mistress. *Ill. 105* Racine wrote only one comedy, *Les Plaideurs*, based on Aristophanes' *Wasps*. Of his nine tragedies, the finest, apart from *Phèdre*, is probably *Britannicus*, which is still in the repertory of the Comédie-Française.

Racine was fortunate in writing for a theatre that had several established companies rivalling each other in splendour and in the excellence of their acting. But his growing reputation suffered at the hands of a vicious cabal, who puffed to success a play by a second-rate dramatist, also on the subject of Phaedra, while causing Racine's to fail on its first production. The resentment he felt, coupled with the offer of a lucrative post at the Court of Louis XIV and perhaps some belated scruples resulting from a rigid upbringing, caused him to abandon the theatre at the height of his powers. His only subsequent dramatic works were the tender and poetic Biblical plays *Esther* and *Athalie*, written at the request of Mme de Maintenon for performance at Saint-Cyr, the convent school she had founded for the daughters of impecunious noblemen.

One of the first people to encourage Racine in his theatrical career *Ills. 108, 111* was Molière, the greatest comic dramatist of France, and perhaps, with the exception of Aristophanes, of the European theatre. The son of a minor Court official, he was educated at a Jesuit college where he was a fellow-pupil of the Prince de Conti, later his patron, and Cyrano de Bergerac. He may have taken part in the performances for which Jesuit schools were renowned, and this, together with a

104

104 Mlle Champmeslé (1642–98), the first
leading lady of the Comédie-Française

105–6 Engravings from a 1676 edition of
Racine's plays show (*left*) a scene from his only
comedy, *Les Plaideurs*, 1668, based on
Aristophanes' *Wasps*; (*right*) *Bérénice*, based on
a passage in Suetonius, and first performed
at the Hôtel de Bourgogne in 1670 with
Mlle Champmeslé (*Ill. 104*) in the leading role

friendship formed with a family of actors named Béjart, probably turned his thoughts to the theatre. After a half-hearted attempt to study law, he left home at the age of twenty-one and dropped his real name of Jean-Baptiste Poquelin in favour of Molière. He made his first appearances with the Béjarts and some of their friends in a converted tennis-court in Paris – the shape of the room used for the game of tennis made it easily adaptable for theatrical purposes, as can be seen from the existing one at Hampton Court, near London, and many French tennis-courts were used in this way. Unfortunately L'Illustre-Théâtre, as it was called, was not a success, and Molière went with his friends into the provinces to lead the usual life of the itinerant actor of the time. For over thirteen years the company, of which he soon became the director, toured France, acting in

Ill. 107 improvised farces in *commedia dell'arte* style (many of them adapted by Molière himself) and gaining valuable experience, until on 24 October 1658, a date memorable in French theatre history, it appeared at the Louvre before Louis XIV and his Court. A tragedy was coolly received, but when the actors appeared in one of Molière's own comedies, now lost, they proved irresistible, and soon found themselves settled in Paris, sharing a theatre with a *commedia dell'arte* troupe, and paying rent to its leader Tiberio Fiorillo, known as

107 Clowns fighting, an illustration from a treatise on theatrical dancing, 1716. This scene of one clown beating another is common in *commedia dell'arte* scenarios, and as a piece of 'comic business' it passed into French comedy and probably into the early plays of Molière

108 Molière (1622–73) as ▶ Caesar in Corneille's *La Mort de Pompée*, in 1659, a portrait by Paul Mignard

109 An open-air performance of Molière's *Le Malade Imaginaire* at Versailles, 1674, given before the King and his Court. The very large stage, splendidly decorated

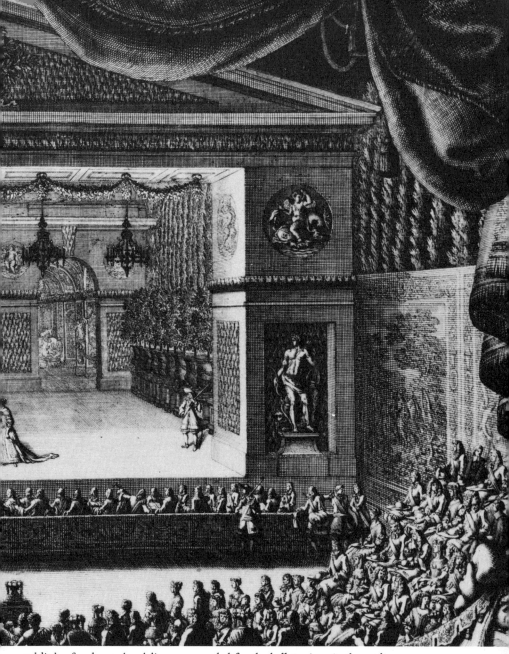

and lit by five large chandeliers, was needed for the ballets given in the prologue
and between the acts

110 Armande Béjart, Molière's wife, in *Psyché*, 1670, a *tragédie-ballet*, written by Molière in collaboration with Corneille (*see Ills. 101–3*) and Philippe Quinault, with music by Jean-Baptiste Lully. The first performance was given in January 1671 in the Salle des Spectacles in the Tuileries, built by Vigarani, before Louis XIV and his Court

111 (*right*) A scene from *Les Femmes Savantes*, in which Molière ridiculed the cult of learning among would-be fashionable ladies. This engraving of 1682 shows the single set in which the play took place, replacing the older simultaneous setting of the Hôtel de Bourgogne (*see Ill. 97*). On stage Chrysale (played by Molière) is remonstrating with his wife Philaminte for dismissing the maid Martine merely because her speech is ungrammatical. The play was first produced at the Palais-Royal in March 1672

Scaramouche. The two leading actors got on very well together, and Molière was always ready to acknowledge how much he learned from the Italians. He was at first forced to adapt his productions to their set scene of houses round a square, reminiscent of Serlio's scene for comedy. Later, when both companies moved from the Petit-Bourbon to the Palais-Royal, he had ample space for his scenery and orchestra – and by then the Italians were paying him rent, so quickly had he advanced in his profession.

From the moment he settled in Paris until his death fifteen years later, at the early age of fifty-one, Molière's life was bound up with *Ill. 110* his theatre. He even married an actress in his company, Armande, the youngest member of the Béjart family, twenty years his junior. It was an unhappy marriage, but it was for Armande that Molière wrote some of his best women's parts, including Elmire in *Tartuffe*,

Célimène in *Le Misanthrope*, Armande in *Les Femmes Savantes*, Elise in *L'Avare*, and above all Lucille in *Le Bourgeois Gentilhomme*. In these plays and in many others Molière and his company appeared *Ill. 111* with almost unbroken success. He was also responsible for several sumptuous entertainments given at Versailles and for plays acted at Court. But it was on the stage of the Palais-Royal that he made his last appearance, in *Le Malade Imaginaire*, on 17 February 1673, dying a few hours later.

Molière's great achievement was that by his own efforts he raised French comedy to the level of French tragedy. Unlike those who had gone before him, and whose comedies were often translated from or based on Italian and particularly Spanish plays, he put down roots in French soil and wrote his plays from his own observations of life around him. His characters are contemporary and French to the backbone, recognizable as such even by spectators of other countries and later ages. This is one of the reasons why his plays defy translation. They can be adapted, as they have been constantly and often with success – by Miles Malleson in England, by Lady Gregory, with her Kiltartan Molière, in Ireland. But it is only the letter which remains. The spirit has evaporated.

During his lifetime Molière saw many changes in the theatre, some of which he helped to bring about. The most important was probably the change-over from the old simultaneous multiple setting used in the Bible-histories and bequeathed to the secular theatre to the single all-purpose set which helped, in tragedy, to preserve the unity of place. In comedy it was probably adopted under the influence of the *commedia dell'arte*, whose peripatetic life made them adepts at simplification. France also came under the influence of Italian scene-designers with their painted scenery and elaborate machinery, used by Molière *Ill. 103* for productions like *Andromède* and *Psyché*, and later snapped up by Lully for his operas and ballets.

Molière, who is the supreme example of the dedicated 'man of the theatre', combining in himself the functions of actor, manager and dramatist, was not only a writer and player of comedy, but provides the connecting link between France's two finest writers of classical tragedy. He first appeared in Paris in *Nicomède*, by Corneille, whom he much admired, and he put on at his own theatre Racine's first play, *La Thébaïde, ou les frères ennemis*. After his death the brilliance of the French theatre was somewhat dimmed. But he left an imperishable memory, for his company, under the management of his widow and her second husband, also an actor, was amalgamated by Louis XIV with two other companies to form the Comédie-Française, the national theatre of France. Its other name is La Maison de Molière, whose traditions it continues to uphold.

CHAPTER SIX

The English Restoration Theatre

While Charles II was in exile he and his followers had become accustomed to watching plays staged in the style used before 1642 for English Court masques, with actresses, painted scenery and machinery imported from Italy, and a proscenium arch with a curtain. It is therefore not surprising that when he returned to England in 1660, he should have encouraged their adoption in the new public theatres. Everything favoured a fresh start, with exciting innovations. The old theatres, after eighteen years of neglect, were unusable. The companies that had played in them were disbanded, the audiences dispersed. The old plays too were out of date. Even Shakespeare was barbarous, and had to be tailored to fit the new age. Many of the perversions of his plays which later appeared in transla-tion on the Continent were really due to rewritings by Restoration dramatists, who dressed up *Macbeth* with singing witches, added new characters to *The Tempest* and gave *Romeo and Juliet* a happy ending.

The two men to whom Charles II by Royal Patents gave the task of reviving the theatre were Thomas Killigrew and William Davenant. Both had been active as playwrights before 1642, and had seen their plays produced in the private theatres which had already begun to feel the influence of Continental staging. Davenant, more-over, who was the godson – some said the illegitimate son – of Shakespeare, had helped in the preparation of Court masques, and in *Ills. 86–8* 1654 had managed to stage in London a 'play with music' now considered the first English opera. This made for continuity, as did the fact that some of the actors in Killigrew's company had had some experience of acting, even if only in the short drolls fashioned, *Ill. 89* like *Bottom the Weaver* from *A Midsummer Night's Dream*, out of old plays, an activity which had sometimes landed them in prison.

The new theatres showed an interesting mixture of English and Continental practices. Roofed like Blackfriars, they retained a *Ill. 85*

memory of the Elizabethan platform-stage in the form of an apron
or forestage. But behind the apron-stage was a proscenium arch with
a window opening into a music-room above it. The arch framed the
painted flats, and the back shutters running in grooves which replaced
the former solid back wall. These back shutters could be opened or
closed to indicate a change of scene – a practice which seems to have
been peculiar to the English stage, and may be a survival of the
medieval use of the unlocalized *platea*. Another feature which was
destined to linger on in English theatres for over two hundred years
was the door opening on the forestage on each side of the proscenium
arch. These – there could be as many as three each side – were known
as the Doors of Entrance. They enabled actors to come and go without using the space behind the arch, which some authorities think
corresponds to the inner stage of the Elizabethan theatre.

    Other innovations in the Restoration theatre were the new
audiences, the plays they came to see, and above all the use of
actresses in female parts. These charming, talented young women,
who replaced the Elizabethan boy-actors, seemed to come from

Ill. 112

112 A scene from Settle's *The Empress of Morocco*, produced at Dorset Garden Theatre in 1673. This theatre was noted for it sumptuous scenery and mechanical devices, many of them copied from the Salle des Spectacles in Paris. It was built under the patent granted by Charles II to Sir William Davenant, its manager

113 A portrait of Nell Gwynne, from the studio of Lely, *c.* 1675. She made her first appearance on the stage at Drury Lane at fifteen, and was excellent in comedy. Her short but spectacular career included playing Florimel in Dryden's *Secret Love* (1667) in male attire. She retired from the theatre to become the mistress of Charles II

nowhere; and with no training, but with abundant self-confidence, they took London by storm. Almost from the beginning they achieved and maintained a high standard and founded a tradition of great acting which continues to this day. One of the best known of these early actresses, though known not so much for her work in the theatre as for the fact that she became the mistress of Charles II, was Nell Gwynne, of Killigrew's company. Others, like Mrs Knipp and Mrs Betterton, are immortalized in Pepys's diary, a storehouse of information on the theatre of his day. *Ill. 113*

Equally revolutionary were the plays written for the new playhouses, and the audiences which came to see them. The Patents under which Killigrew and Davenant operated are still in force. One belongs to Drury Lane Theatre, which now stands near the site of Killigrew's first Theatre Royal of 1663, built over a riding yard. *Ill. 125* The other controls Covent Garden Opera House, inheritor of the traditions of Davenant's Duke's House in Lincoln's Inn Fields, and his later Dorset Garden Theatre. Since the Patents created a monopoly of acting, London now had only two theatres instead of the ten or *Ill. 112* twelve of Elizabethan times. The audience, composed of fashionable young men and their hangers-on, and women of the town, was small, cynical and restless, eager to be seen and heard, avid for something new, equally intolerant of poetry and of homespun comedy. For a time they had to be content with refurbishings of old plays, and their taste may be gauged by the fact that they preferred Beaumont and Fletcher to Shakespeare and Ben Jonson. But soon they had their own playwrights, who inaugurated the bawdy comedy of manners which is known as Restoration comedy, though it continued as late as 1707, under Queen Anne. It began harmlessly enough with Etherege, took on a sharper edge with Wycherley, and reached its zenith in the works of Congreve and Vanbrugh, ending with the

114 The Closet Scene from *Hamlet*, an engraving of 1709 showing the Restoration manner of staging – the Hamlet may be intended for Betterton. Two points illustrated became traditional – the overturned chair and Hamlet's stocking, as Ophelia said (II. 1), 'ungartered and down-gyved'

115 John Rich, manager of
the first Covent Garden
Theatre, as Harlequin, 1731,
a print satirizing the vogue
for the harlequinade
and the ballad-opera

boisterous and high-spirited plays of Farquhar. It depicts a world of inverted moral values, of cuckoldry and intrigue, in which the wit of the fortune-hunter is more highly prized than romance or common sense. Its finest memorial is Congreve's *Way of the World*, which is intellectual comedy at its best. Other writers of the revived comedy of humours, like Shadwell, or of the comedies of intrigue taken from Spanish sources, were shrewd observers of contemporary life and very popular in their own day, but they are mostly forgotten, except perhaps for Mrs Aphra Behn, notable as the first woman to earn her living by playwriting, and incidentally a Government spy and the introducer of milk punch into England.

The drama of the Restoration period was not however confined to comedy. It had its tragic moments, particularly with Dryden's heroic plays, which endeavoured to acclimatize the trappings of French neo-classicism in England, without success. More to the taste of the time, and still acceptable in revival, was Otway's *Venice Preserved*, in which the leading actor of the Restoration stage, and its first Hamlet, Thomas Betterton, appeared with Mrs Barry, as outstanding in tragedy as Mrs Bracegirdle was in comedy. When Betterton in 1695 produced Congreve's *Love for Love*, Mrs Bracegirdle played Angelica to Betterton's Valentine.

Ill. 114

Love for Love was produced at the Lincoln's Inn Fields Theatre where John Rich was later to stage Gay's *Beggar's Opera*. Rich, who was also responsible for the building of the first Covent Garden

Ill. 115

Theatre, is an important figure in the development of the English stage. Under the name of Lun he appeared as Harlequin in the 'Italian Night Scenes' imported from France. These vestiges of the *commedia dell'arte* featured Harlequin metamorphosed, as in *Harlequin Doctor Faustus* or *Harlequin Jack Sheppard*, and provided one of the elements of that uniquely English entertainment, the Christmas pantomime, which within living memory always ended with a Harlequinade.

The early eighteenth century saw many changes in the style of the English theatre building. The typically Georgian playhouse, of which the first was Potter's Little Theatre in the Haymarket, was less influenced by the Italian opera-house than theatres elsewhere, perhaps because the English theatrical genius remained obstinately dramatic rather than operatic. Potter's theatre, and many which were later *Ill. 117* built in the same style, was a soberly elegant little building, with tiers of boxes rising directly from the pit, and proscenium doors opening on to an attenuated forestage. Scenery was still painted on the flat. The lighting was by overhead chandeliers with wax or tallow candles, and the curtain in the proscenium arch rose and fell only at the beginning and end of the play. In 1730 an important innovation took place when the orchestra moved to a well in front of the stage.

The audience was by now becoming more numerous but less sophisticated, and it demanded not only the ubiquitous afterpiece, introduced as a sop to those who came in late at half-price, but sentiment instead of comedy and pathos in the place of tragedy. The *Ill. 116* first play in the new style, *Love's Last Shift*, was by Colley Cibber, playwright and for a long time manager of Drury Lane, whose best play was probably *The Careless Husband*. An egregious fop and a very poor Poet Laureate, Cibber is now remembered for his memoirs and for his adaptation of *Richard III*, which contained the oft-quoted lines: 'Off with his head! So much for Buckingham!' and 'Now Richard is himself again.' It remained the standard acting text of the play for over a century and a half.

The sentimentality of *Love's Last Shift* had one good result, since it goaded the architect Vanbrugh, who not only built the Queen's

118

116 Colley Cibber as Lord Foppington in Vanbrugh's *The Relapse; or Virtue in Danger*, 1696

117 The interior of the Regency Theatre, Tottenham Street, London, as it was in 1817 during a performance of *Othello*, and probably very much earlier. It shows the typical eighteenth-century auditorium with boxes at stage level rising directly from the pit, and two elegant balconies

Theatre in the Haymarket but also provided plays for it, into writing his best comedy, the savagely satiric *The Relapse*, in which, ironically enough, Cibber gave one of his finest performances as *Ill. 116* Lord Foppington. But the tide was running too strongly in favour of *bourgeois* tragedy and domestic drama for any one person to stem it. A long period of mediocrity set in which led in the 1770s to the mawkish plays of which Cumberland's *The Brothers* and Kelly's *False Delicacy* are typical, and against which Goldsmith and Sheridan reacted so strongly.

The theatres of London naturally set the pattern for the many small playhouses which were erected in the provinces in the eighteenth century. The only remaining examples are the Theatres Royal at Bristol, Margate and Richmond (Yorks.), all much restored. England, being strongly centred on London, and ruled by a dynasty with little interest in playgoing, never had those princely or ducal theatres which were scattered all over Europe, and can still be seen

118 The Tankard Street Theatre, Ipswich, where David Garrick made his first appearance in 1741 under Henry Giffard, an engraving from Wilkinson's *Theatrum Illustrata*, 1825

119 David Garrick and his wife, Eva Maria Viegel, dancer at the Haymarket under the name of Mme Violetta, whom he married in 1749. Garrick was the leading figure of the English stage from 1741 to 1776

at Drottningholm in Sweden, at Celle in Germany, at Český Krumlov in Czechoslovakia, and even in the restored palaces of Soviet Russia. Nor could many towns support a theatre all the year round. They were visited by travelling companies whose journeys in the 1720s and 1730s fell into a pattern which soon resolved itself into a circuit. Each company then had its own territory, made up of towns which could easily be reached from a large centre. Of the many provincial managers of the time the best known are Tate Wilkinson of the York circuit, and Sarah Baker, who covered the whole of Kent. These stock companies were the training-ground of many fine players, for the eighteenth century, which was an age of poor playwriting, was strong in acting talent. The greatest actor of the day was undoubtedly David Garrick, who had his training on the *Ill. 119* Ipswich circuit under Giffard. Equally effective in tragedy and *Ill. 118* comedy, he radically changed the style of English acting, substituting freedom of movement and natural delivery for the stiffness and *Ill. 128* pomposity of such older actors as Quin. Of medium height, but well proportioned, with expressive, flashing eyes and exceptionally mobile features, he appeared in many modern plays, some of which he wrote himself, and also in revivals of Shakespeare. He was responsible for many improvements in the theatre, and in 1765 introduced stage lighting concealed from the audience, producing an effect which can *Ill. 125* be studied in the engraving of *The School for Scandal*. He also removed the spectators who had hitherto encumbered the stage, and created something of a sensation with the splendid cut-out and romantic scenery designed for him by the Continental stage-designer de *Ill. 120* Louterbourg. His career ran triumphantly from his début as Richard

120 A 'cut-out' scene by de Louterbourg, a painter from Alsace who became scenic director at Drury Lane under Garrick and later under Sheridan, making important reforms in lighting effects and scenery. His fires, storms, volcanoes and cloud-effects were much admired

III in 1741 to his retirement in 1776. Most of his time was spent at Drury Lane, where his leading ladies included Peg Woffington, his *Ill. 121* mistress for many years, who reversed Elizabethan theatre practice by appearing in young men's parts, and Kitty Clive, an excellent *Ill. 122* actress in comedy who was much admired by Horace Walpole.

Garrick's only rival in his own day was Macklin, best remembered for having rescued Shylock from the clutches of the low comedian and played him as a tragic and dignified figure. This drew from *Ill. 123* Pope the memorable, though not perhaps strictly accurate, couplet: 'This is the Jew/That Shakespeare drew'. Macklin also discarded the scarlet of the king's livery in which Garrick still played Macbeth, and appeared for the first time in something approximating to the 'old

121 (*left*) Peg Woffington as Mistress Ford in *The Merry Wives of Windsor*, in a painting of 1751

122 (*right*) Kitty Clive as Isabella in Fielding's *The Old Debauchees*, in 1750

123 (*left*) Charles Macklin as Shylock at Drury Lane, 1741. He dressed soberly instead of wearing rags, and spoke naturally in contrast to the ranting of Quin as Antonio (*see Ill. 128*). His Portia was Kitty Clive (*see Ill. 122*), who convulsed the audience in the Trial Scene by mimicking well-known barristers of the time

124 (*right*) Ned Shuter and Mrs Green as Mr and Mrs Hardcastle, and John Quick as Tony Lumpkin in Goldsmith's *She Stoops to Conquer*, from an engraving after Parkinson. The play was first produced at Covent Garden in 1773. The costumes are interesting, but for a view of a contemporary stage, see Drury Lane in *Ill. 125*

Caledonian habit'. Garrick replied by dressing *King Lear* in accordance with his own ideas of 'old English costume'. Neither attempt, it is fair to say, was particularly remarkable for authenticity.

Garrick's success inevitably made him many enemies, of whom the bitterest was Samuel Foote. This excellent actor took over the Haymarket in 1747, and managed by various subterfuges to evade the Licensing Act of 1737. This had been hurriedly passed under Walpole in an effort to restrain the satiric attacks on the Government by Henry Fielding, at the same theatre. Its chief result had been to drive Fielding from the theatre to novel-writing, but it had also confirmed the monopoly of Drury Lane and Covent Garden, and hindered the expansion of the smaller unlicensed theatres. Foote, who eventually managed to get permission to open the Haymarket in

the summer when the Patent theatres were closed, was also a satirist, who made himself universally feared and admired by his mordant wit and cruel mimicry. He wrote most of his own material, and excelled in brilliant but ephemeral sketches of contemporary manners which caused him to be nicknamed 'the English Aristophanes'.

Garrick was succeeded in the management of Drury Lane by Sheridan, who in spite of his preoccupation with politics gave much of his time to the theatre. With Goldsmith he represents the revolt of the reasonable man against the excesses of sensibility. The robust humour of Goldsmith's *She Stoops to Conquer* derives from Shake- *Ill. 124* speare and the Elizabethans, that of Sheridan's *The Rivals* and *The School for Scandal* from Congreve and Restoration comedy, with as much wit but less licence. Both of Sheridan's plays have remained in the repertory of the English theatre, *The Rivals* offering an excellent role for a low comedian in Bob Acres, first played at Covent Garden in 1775 by Quick, and *The School for Scandal* two equally good high-comedy roles in Sir Peter and Lady Teazle, first played at Drury Lane in 1777 by Tom King and Mrs Abington.

Ill. 125

Goldsmith wrote nothing more for the theatre, though his novel, *The Vicar of Wakefield*, dramatized a hundred years later, provided a charming vehicle for Ellen Terry. Sheridan's later plays included *A Trip to Scarborough*, a rewriting for a more squeamish age of Vanbrugh's *The Relapse*, in which the celebrated Mrs Jordan played

125 The Screen Scene from Sheridan's *School for Scandal*, with Tom King and Mrs Abington as Sir Peter and Lady Teazle. This engraving gives an excellent idea of Drury Lane in 1777. Built in 1672, it was extensively altered by the Adam brothers in 1775. The shaft of light coming from the wings on the actors' left confirms the use of side-lighting at this date

Miss Hoyden; *The Critic*, a burlesque of heroic drama which is still effective on the stage; and a pantomime, *Robinson Crusoe*. In 1794 Sheridan replaced the much-altered theatre of 1674, which was in poor condition, by a much larger building designed by Holland. There, pandering to the prevailing taste for spectacle and pantomime, he continued the profligate course that almost brought the theatre to bankruptcy, and drove his best actors to Covent Garden. He also indulged in constant litigation with the managers of the unlicensed theatres, whose success alarmed him, particularly Astley's, famous for its equestrian shows, Sadler's Wells under the management of *Ill. 126*

126 Anglers outside Sadler's Wells Theatre, 1796, a drawing by Cruikshank. This theatre, which later came into prominence under Phelps (*see Ill. 191*), was built by Rosoman on the site of a former concert-hall near a medicinal spring. A second Sadler's Wells on the same site was opened in 1931 by Lilian Baylis, and is at present used for opera

Tom King, and the Royalty under John Palmer, both fugitive actors from Drury Lane.

Another actor, destined to play a big part in English theatrical history, who preferred to disassociate himself from Sheridan's ruinous policy was John Philip Kemble, who with his sister, Mrs Siddons, moved to Covent Garden in 1802. Here one of Kemble's first acts as manager was to engage the remarkable 'Young Roscius', Master Betty, a thirteen-year-old tragedian who surpassed even Mrs Siddons in popularity. He had a great vogue, and it is said that when he appeared as Hamlet Parliament was adjourned on a motion of the younger Pitt in order that the members might attend his performance. As an adult actor, however, he had no success, and passed the rest of his long life – he was well over eighty when he died – in complete obscurity.

Ill. 127

In September 1808 Covent Garden was burnt to the ground. Five months later Drury Lane suffered the same fate. It was the end of an epoch. The new buildings which arose on both sites, vast white elephants which were to break the hearts of actors and managers alike, ushered in a new phase in the history of the English theatre.

127 Master Betty ('The Young Roscius') as Hamlet, 1804

CHAPTER SEVEN

The Theatre in Eighteenth-century Germany

The reforms in costume attempted by Macklin and Garrick in London in the 1770s were not the first tentatives in this direction. In Germany the first break with tradition came as early as 1741, when the reformer and theatre critic Gottsched persuaded Carolina Neuber, leader of the company which was to perform his Roman tragedy, *Der sterbende Cato*, to put her actors into classical dress, with disastrous results. Perhaps the quest for too high a degree of accuracy is anti-theatrical, and costume, in becoming historical, ceases to have a history of its own. Certainly an earlier urge towards authenticity would have deprived the theatre of the work of many designers whose fantastic inventions,.intended for Court masques, operas, and other spectacular entertainments, nevertheless spilled over into the ordinary playhouses and enlivened many a dull play. They even, at times, influenced the fashion of the outside world, as did the designs of Bérain, one of the greatest artists in stage costuming, under Louis XIV, or those of François Boucher under Louis XV. The latter's wide-panniered skirt with rococo details, familiar in the theatres of the whole of Europe, reached as far as London, where it was worn by Quin as Coriolanus.

Ill. 138

Ill. 128

The reference to Carolina Neuber, or Die Neuberin, as she was called, indicates that Germany is now making a determined if somewhat belated appearance on the European theatrical scene. Several factors had combined to hinder the development of an indigenous German theatre, among them constant warfare, religious faction, the overpowering influence of visiting French and Italian companies, and above all the lack of a focal point like that provided for France and England by their capital cities. Actors and playwrights were thus deprived of that close contact with a tightly-knit society which produced the pungent satire of the French *sotie* and the charm of the English interlude. Nor was the acrobatic agility of the Italian

comedians or the religious fervour of the Spanish *autos*, both from
countries with no focal point, within the compass of the German
theatre at that time. The characteristic personage of early German
Ill. 129 farce is the *Narr*, or Fool, in his cap and bells, who, though he began
as a Court jester, has affinities both with the comic devil of the Bible-
history and the sly *zanni* of the *commedia dell'arte* – but only such as
are common to all comedians, and not necessarily attributable to
outside influences. Even the tide of the new learning had little effect
on the German theatre, and the best plays, of little interest today,
were those written in support of the Reformation and the Counter-
Reformation. These, even when designed to reinforce the Protestant
argument, were still performed in the old medieval (and therefore
Catholic) simultaneous setting. The secular farces – there was as yet
no serious secular drama in Germany – had been taken over by the

130

128 (*left*) The tragic hero in plumes and panniered skirt. James Quin (1693–1766) as Coriolanus in the play of that name by James Thomson, at Covent Garden in 1749

129 (*right*) A German Fool, or *Narr*, in cap and bells, end of the fifteenth century. This engraving shows Claus Narr, court jester to the Electors of Saxony between 1461 and 1518, strangling his goslings to save them from drowning

130–1 Scenes from a School Drama by Johann Rasser, 1574. The open-air platform stage, probably erected in a market-place, is very like the Terence stage (*see Ills. 45–9*), with a curtained booth and the audience on three sides. (*above*) A mother protects her son from his irate tutor while a second child, his satchel over his shoulder, makes for the exit. (*below*) A dispute between two peasants

guilds of Mastersingers, and could therefore be staged a little more
Ills. 130, 131 lavishly than when they had been given by groups of amateurs on
Ills. 132, 133 temporary platform-stages. But even the plays of Hans Sachs, well
known to opera-goers through his appearance in Wagner's *Die
Meistersinger von Nürnberg*, were presented very simply (in the 1550s)
on an improvised stage in Nuremberg's abandoned Marthakirche.
This constituted Germany's first theatre building, with the audience
in the body of the church facing a raised stage curtained at the back
and sides. Existing steps and the pulpit were pressed into service, and
the actors, no longer visible throughout the play as in earlier productions, came and went through gaps in the curtains, carrying with them
the props and stage furniture which the action called for. The general
Ill. 48 effect must have been something like that of the Terence-stage.
Sachs, who wrote with great facility in a not unpleasing doggerel
four-beat line, composed some long academic tragedies and comedies,
usually on classical or Biblical themes, so it is reasonable to suppose
that he was acquainted with the Terence-stage. But his fame rests
mainly on his short Carnival plays, which turned the rough humour
of the original *Fastnachtsspiel* into a simple folk-tale, purging it of
indecency without discarding its sense of fun. Though his plays are
not very original, they are marked by many deft touches, a sense of
characterization, and some feeling for dramatic effect. They were
produced by the author who also trained the actors in what seems to
have been a fairly realistic style. Costuming was simple, consisting of
traditional robes for divine and noble personages, and everyday dress
Ill. 132 for lesser mortals.

It was, curiously enough, the wandering troupes of English actors
– the *Englische Komödianten* – who had the greatest influence on the
nascent German-speaking theatre, both in Austria and in Germany.
The first of these companies, under Robert Browne, appeared at
Frankfurt in 1592, and shortly afterwards a company under Sackville
was established at Wolfenbüttel in the Court Theatre of Heinrich
Julius of Brunswick. The Duke was himself a playwright. His extant
plays show considerable English influence, having in them much
that can be traced to Shakespeare, as well as some affinities with the
commedia dell'arte.

132

Der Teuffel left kepn
Zantzknecht mehr inn die
helle faren.

Hans Sachs.

132–3 (*right*) An early German dramatist, the mastersinger Hans Sachs (1494–1576), a cobbler by profession, and (*left*) a woodcut from the title-page of one of his plays

There are scattered mentions of other English companies in the early seventeenth century. They played at the big annual fairs, in noblemen's halls, or in the larger towns, either indoors or out. Some of them even penetrated into Scandinavia. As they travelled light, their scenery must have been non-existent, and the stages erected locally for them were modifications of the normal Elizabethan structure. They consisted of a large jutting-out platform with a room at the back and perhaps a gallery above. This allowed of greater mobility than the long narrow stage of the Marthakirche, and the actors took full advantage of it, playing with all the agility of contemporary London actors, reinforced by the acrobatics of the *commedia dell'arte*. The repertory consisted mainly of Elizabethan comedies and tragedies, often severely cut, played in English with the help of music, dancing and dumbshow, and enlivened between the acts by the patter in Low German of the Fool. This all-pervasive character found his way even into the burlesque version of *Hamlet*,

133

which as *Die bestrafte Brudermord* later became one of the most popular pieces in the repertory of the German travelling companies. The Fool, though of English origin, quickly absorbed some of the characteristics of the German *Narr*, and was played by Sackville as Jan Clant (Clown) or Bouschet (Posset), by Robert Reynolds as Pickelherring, and by John Spencer as Hans Stockfisch.

The influence of the English Comedians was no doubt deplorable from a literary point of view, and led to the later popularity of the crude plays of bloody deeds in high places – the *Haupt- und Staats-*
Ill. 139 *aktionen* – but by their productions they accustomed the public to action and passion on the stage, and helped to curb the tendency of German dramatists to excessive discussion. For them the play was indeed the thing, and in ramming that point home they revolutionized German drama. Even after German troupes had taken over the work of the English companies, their name remained useful for publicity purposes, being synonymous with all that was most admired and successful in the theatre. Their activities were hampered by the Thirty Years War, but they appeared in Germany again during the English Puritan interregnum which drove them from London. The constant passage of actors to and from the Continent must have led to a good deal of cross-fertilization in the theatre, and has posed some interesting problems in comparative literature, outside the scope of this book, of which the use made of the Faustus legend both in England and in Germany is a case in point. The last English troupe in Germany is mentioned in 1659, by which time popular staging had
Ill. 134 begun to feel the influence of Italian perspective scenery. This came in by way of the elaborate Court spectacles, mostly operatic, given in theatres built for the reigning princes by Italian architects, and also through the splendidly staged Jesuit school plays, with texts in Latin,
Ill. 136 which were dominated by Italian scenery and machinery. There was as yet no permanent public theatre in Germany where the plays of her first serious dramatist, Andreas Gryphius, could be seen, and they were performed by Protestant schoolboys. Based on French classical drama, they were written in lofty and somewhat monotonous verse, and would probably not have been well received by an audience which still delighted in the *Haupt- und Staatsaktionen*, whose

134

extempore productions retained many of the faults of the English Comedians without their virtues. These were particularly popular in Vienna, and it was not long before the local form of the fool, Hanswurst, who seems to have evolved from John Posset (alias *Ill. 135* Johann Guttwen), ousted all the earlier imported forms. In the hands of the actor Stranitzky, Hanswurst became a completely original comic figure. Discarding the earlier loose white belted tunic and trousers, reminiscent of the costume of Pedrolino, he was dressed like a peasant from Salzburg, in a loose red jacket with a small fool's ruff, yellow pantaloons held up by red braces, a blue heart on his chest embroidered with the initials H. W., a tufted wig, a beard, heavy eyebrows, and a green pointed hat. He dominated most of the plays in the repertory of the Kärntnertor, the first permanent home of German-language comedy, and in the hands of Stranitzky's successor Prehauser underwent a mellowing process which corresponded to the alteration in the plays themselves, from improvised farces to a more sophisticated portrayal of recognizable Viennese types. Two later comic figures of the Viennese folk-play were Kasperle, the puppet-theatre equivalent of the English Punch, and Thaddädl. The latter, who belonged to a very different age and theatre from that of Hanswurst, was a falsetto-voiced, clumsy, infantile booby, perpetually infatuated. The plays in which he appeared were no longer improvisations, but texts specially written for him, or rather for the actor who immortalized him, Anton Hasenhut.

In the early eighteenth century efforts were made by serious-minded persons, both in Germany and in Austria, to banish the old comedies in favour of something more dignified, and to replace the pre-eminence of the professional actor, who had been paramount in the German theatre of the seventeenth century, by that of the literary dramatist. The reformer Gottsched, whose work was not confined *Ill. 137* to the theatre, particularly detested the improvised plays centred on a debased Harlequinade, with their rowdy foolery and easily satisfied audiences. Helped by the intrepid Carolina Neuber, he was *Ill. 138* successful for a time in banishing Harlequin from the stage and in replacing him and his antics by sober works in the French classical manner, written in prosaic alexandrines. Unfortunately Gottsched

134 (*above*) A seventeenth-century
German stage, with wings, backcloth and hanging chandeliers, but
no footlights. The play is a
romantic or chevalresque comedy,
the winged cupid at the back
presaging a happy ending

135 The English actor John
Goodwin as Hanswurst, a stage in
the development of the German
clown showing the influence of the
English Comedians in the
seventeenth century

136

136 (*above*) The splendour of the Jesuit school productions: the arrival of Neptune, from *Pietas Victrix* by Nicolaus Avancinus, Vienna, 1659. The play had forty-six speaking parts and called for a large crowd of supers in addition

137 The German critic and dramatist Johann Christoph Gottsched (1700–66), and his wife Luise Adelgunde Victoria *née* Kulman (1713–62), who together translated and adapted a number of French classical plays for the company of Carolina Neuber (*see Ill. 138*)

138 The first outstanding German actress and theatre manageress, Carolina Neuber (1697–1760), seen here as Elizabeth I of England in a translation into German of Thomas Corneille's *Essex*. Neuber's efforts to reform the German stage failed to oust the *Haupt- und Staatsaktionen* (*Ill. 139*) from popular favour

was working in a style which was already out of date. The result was dull and did not last long. By the middle of the eighteenth century translations of Shakespeare's plays had opened up a new world of the imagination to the German playgoer, who had also become aware of the success on the contemporary French stage of the *comédie larmoyante* and the *drame bourgeois*. But Gottsched's influence had not been wholly bad. The discipline he sought to impose on the inchoate stage of his time was salutary, and his conception of the theatre as a civic institution was to bear fruit later on.

The chief opponent of Gottsched was the young Lessing, who acquired his knowledge of the theatre backstage with the company

139 A troupe of itinerant German actors getting ready to appear in a *Haupt- und Staatsaktion* in Nuremberg, *c.* 1730; an engraving by P. Decker. These were plays dealing with dramatic events in high places, with comic interludes supplied by Harlequin and Hanswurst (seen on the extreme left)

of Carolina Neuber. She produced his first comedies, which were written in the style of Molière, whom he much admired. But his first important work, *Miss Sara Sampson*, is a domestic tragedy clearly influenced by Richardson's novels, then very popular in Germany.

Lessing, whose work as a dramatic critic is no less important than his plays, was connected in 1765 with one of the first attempts to establish a permanent national theatre in Hamburg, where his *Minna von Barnhelm*, the first masterpiece of German comedy, was acted in 1767. The Hamburg venture, which was doomed to failure, was headed by two remarkable men, Ackermann and Ekhof, who had a great influence on the German theatre of their day. Ekhof in particular abandoned the wooden declamation and stiff posturing of earlier actors under Carolina Neuber and Koch for the supple and natural style already in vogue elsewhere. Both Ekhof and Ackermann belonged originally to a company led by Schönemann, who had been a harlequin in a travelling troupe, and when his predilection for horse-dealing ruined him, they took over. In the reorganized company were Ackermann's two daughters, both excellent actresses, and a son of Ackermann's wife by a previous marriage, Friedrich *Ill. 140* Schröder. He was one of Germany's greatest actors, and the first to play many of Shakespeare's parts in translation, from Hamlet to King Lear. Unfortunately, Schröder's jealousy of Ekhof caused the latter to leave the company, and for some years he toured unhappily before going first to Weimar, where he met Goethe and may have supplied him with some of the material for *Wilhelm Meister*, and then to Gotha. It was at Gotha that the year before his death he engaged a young actor named Iffland, destined to play an important part in the theatre of Goethe's day. Ekhof lived long enough to see the acting profession in Germany, largely through his own efforts, achieve respectability. The change in status can be judged by the fact that Christian burial, refused to the actor-manager Velten in 1692, was freely accorded to Ekhof in 1778.

After Ackermann's death Schröder who, like Ekhof, appears in *Wilhelm Meister*, with his sister Charlotte (as Serlo and Aurelie), took over the leadership of the company and instituted many reforms, particularly in stage costuming. The period which followed was perhaps the most glorious in his career. As well as revealing the theatrical qualities of Shakespeare's plays to a young audience which knew them only on the printed page, he produced *Emilia Galotti*, by the ageing Lessing, and the first play of the young Goethe, *Götz von Berlichingen*. But in spite of his success he was not happy. Tiring of constant friction with his mother, who still held the purse-strings, he *Ill. 143* left Germany for the Vienna Burgtheater. The four years he spent there made a permanent impression on the Austrian theatre, and he may be said to have inaugurated the subtle and refined style of ensemble playing which later became the hall-mark of a Burgtheater production. It was Schröder too who first trained and guided the

great Brockmann, a leading actor at the Burgtheater from 1778 *Ill. 142*
until his death in 1812.

Schröder's time in Vienna coincided with the efforts of Joseph II to
continue the reforms begun by his mother, the Empress Maria
Theresa, by making the Burgtheater a national home for serious and
improving drama and banishing the popular theatre to the suburbs,
where it flourished more strongly than ever under Marinelli at the
Theater in der Leopoldstadt.

140 Friedrich Schröder (1744–1816), the first interpreter of Shakespeare in
Germany, as Falstaff in a production of 1780. Schröder adapted Shakespeare to
suit the taste of the time, allowing, for example, Hamlet and Cordelia to survive.
Here he wears Elizabethan doublet and hose with the plumed hat of the tragic hero

141 (*right*) Johann Wolfgang Goethe (1749–1832), a portrait by Georg Oswald, 1799. This many-sided genius wrote a number of fine plays, was himself a good amateur actor (*Ill. 144*), and was for many years responsible for the management of the Court Theatre at Weimar (*Ill. 145*)

142 (*far right*) Johann Brockmann (1745–1812) as Hamlet in the Play Scene, in a production in Berlin in 1778 by the company of Karl Döbbelin, one of the best of the period

143 The interior of the first Burg-theater in Vienna, which was situated on the Michaelerplatz, and was built between 1741 and 1756. It is interesting to compare it with the eighteenth-century playhouses of London (*see Ill. 117*) and elsewhere. The elaborately decorated auditorium is three-sided, not horseshoe shaped, and there is a small forestage with boxes instead of the English proscenium doors

144 (*left*) Goethe as
Orestes with Corona
Schroeter as Iphigenia,
in a Court production
of Goethe's *Iphigenie
auf Tauris* at the castle
at Ettersburg in 1779;
a painting by
G. M. Kraus

145 (*right*) The Court ▶
Theatre at Weimar
during the directorship
of Goethe (1784–1825)

The German stage at the end of the eighteenth century was
dominated by Goethe, who devoted part of his abundant genius to the
service of the theatre. His *Götz von Berlichingen* was the first German
play to be written under the influence of Shakespeare. Though he
later reverted to his earlier admiration for French dramatic literature,
his play became the manifesto of the *Sturm und Drang* writers, setting
a pattern which was followed by most of the younger dramatists,
particularly Schiller. Goethe's next dramatic works were historical
and domestic dramas, of which *Clavigo*, with its Spanish setting, still
acts well. But in later life he wrote more as a poet than a dramatist,
with such plays as *Iphigenie auf Tauris* and *Faust*, a cosmic drama in
two parts. It has been staged in its entirety, but in the vastness of its
conception and the strength of its execution it transcends the limits
of the normal playhouse.

Ill. 141

Ill. 146

Ill. 144

144

It was during Goethe's management of the Court Theatre at
Weimar – one of his many official positions there, which from 1799
to 1805 he shared with Schiller – that most of the latter's plays were
staged, from *Wallenstein* to *Wilhelm Tell*. But his first, the epoch-
making *Die Räuber*, had had its première at Mannheim, with Ekhof's
protégé Iffland as Franz Moor. Iffland, who was later to appear at
Weimar with great success, was also a popular playwright, and a
good actor in serious comedy, but not in tragedy, having an excellent
technique but no depth. Luckily he trained his young actors in the
sobriety of Schröder rather than in his own virtuosity, and handed on
many excellent traditions to the actors of the Romantic period,
particularly Ludwig Devrient. The culminating point of his career
came in 1796, when he became director of the National Theatre in
Berlin, where he remained until his death in 1814. He produced a

Ill. 145

146 Friedrich von Schiller (1759–1805), one of Germany's greatest playwrights, a portrait by Anton Graff. From 1799 to his death Schiller was jointly responsible with Goethe for the productions at the Court Theatre in Weimar

Ill. 146

number of old and new plays, among them those of Shakespeare and Schiller, in the grandiose romantic settings which were prepared for him by the architect and designer Schinkel. His actors were accounted better than those of Weimar, where Goethe, in reaction against the brutal realism of the *Sturm und Drang* movement and the naturalism of the *bourgeois* domestic drama, had introduced a more dignified and poetic style of acting. This unfortunately led to some stiffness and declamation, though crowd scenes were still well and realistically handled. But the literary content of Schiller's plays, combined with those of Goethe and Lessing, as well as translations of Shakespeare and Calderón, sufficed for a time to place Weimar's Court Theatre at the forefront of the German theatrical scene.

But even Weimar had to admit the melodramatic plays of Kotzebue, which are a portent of what is to come. The early nineteenth

146

century, inheritor of the turmoil of the French Revolution, with its repercussions all over Europe, was to be once again a period of great acting and poor plays – poor in a literary, not a theatrical sense, for a prodigious amount of work in the way of scenery, costumes, music and stage effects was to go into the production of the melo-dramas and romantic plays which trace their ancestry back to the youthful excesses of *Götz von Berlichingen* and *Die Räuber*, ignoring entirely the later and more restrained excellencies of Goethe's *Torquato Tasso* and Schiller's *Maria Stuart*. In such an atmosphere the plays of a dramatist like Kleist, whether comic, as in *Der zerbrockene Krug*, or heroic, as in *Der Prinz von Homburg*, were bound to be *Ill. 180* unappreciated, and they had to wait to make their effect until audiences were in a more receptive frame of mind.

147 *Die Verschwörung des Fiesko zu Genua*, by Schiller, in a production at the Court Theatre, Weimar, in *c.* 1810. It was first produced in Bonn in 1783 and several times revived

CHAPTER EIGHT

France before the Revolution

While Germany was struggling to establish permanent theatres and develop a national school of play-writing, France was going through a somewhat difficult and barren period. The death of Molière had brought to an end a glorious epoch. The newly established Comédie-Française was in many ways an admirable institution. It had as its *Ills. 110, 104* leading ladies Molière's widow and Mlle Champmeslé, and as its *Ills. 148, 150* leading actors Molière's pupil Baron, famous in tragedy, and Poisson, famous for his portrayal of Crispin, in comedy. But perhaps because it was a little too conscious of its official backing and subsidy, it tended to impose on the French theatre as a whole a traditional style and repertory which brooked no opposition and left very little room for experiment. Maintaining the form without the content, tragedy declined into sensationalism and melodrama, while comedy lost its universal appeal and concerned itself rather too much with contemporary trivialities. Meanwhile, the Italian actors, under their leader *Ill. 149* Giuseppe Biancolelli, known as Dominique, had obtained from Louis XIV, in the teeth of bitter opposition from the Comédie-Française, the right to play in French. They were successful in the plays of Dufresny and Regnard, comedies which allowed them ample scope for impro- *Ill. 152* visation, but in 1697 a fancied slight to Mme de Maintenon caused them to be banished from Paris, and they did not return until after the King's death in 1716, when they again occupied the theatre in the Hôtel de Bourgogne, which had become known as the Comédie-Italienne, to distinguish it from the Comédie-Française, housed since 1689 in d'Orþay's new building. The Italians' acting and repertory alike had become outmoded, but by a process of trial and error they succeeded in recapturing the interest of the public, and in time evolved what was virtually a new form of theatrical art, combining Italian ebullience and dexterity with French wit and elegance. It was this combination of talents which enabled the Italian actors, under

148

148 The actor and playwright Michel Baron (1653–1729), a portrait by Rigaud. Baron was responsible for the early training of Adrienne Lecouvreur (*see Ill. 157*)

149 The leading actor of the Comédie-Italienne, Giuseppe Biancolelli (*c.* 1637–88), known as Dominique, in the costume of Il Dottore

Lelio and the younger Dominique, to interpret so ably the comedies of Marivaux. These, which retained from the *commedia dell'arte* the tradition of using the actor's name for the part he was playing, were all variations on a single theme – that of young people in love, whose difficulties, though momentary and often of their own making, are universally applicable. Action is replaced by psychological insight,   *Ill. 151*

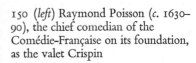

150 (*left*) Raymond Poisson (*c.* 1630–90), the chief comedian of the Comédie-Française on its foundation, as the valet Crispin

151 (*below left*) Actors of the Comédie-Italienne, Paris, where the plays of Pierre de Marivaux (1688–1763) were first given; a painting by Nicolas Lancret

152 (*right*) The Italian actors who were banished from Paris in 1697 after a play entitled *La Fausse Prude* had offended Mme de Maintenon

153 (*below*) French actors, probably those at the Comédie-Française, in a tragedy, *c.* 1720; after Watteau

and the poignancy of the emotional situation is expressed in a paradoxical and slightly precious style which was later labelled *marivaudage* – partly in admiration, partly in reproach, for Marivaux in his own day was not as highly regarded as he is now. He escaped classification, for he belonged to no recognizable stream of tradition, and his style, which seemed so easy and informal, was a trap for the unwary. Few ventured on it, and he left no successors, remaining an isolated phenomenon which arose solely from the acclimatization in France of the transfigured *commedia dell'arte*.

It was a disaster for the Comédie-Française, who were much less successful with Marivaux than their rivals, that one of their ablest

154 (*below*) Actors at the Foire St-Laurent parading in front of a temporary theatre *c.* 1720

155 (*right*) The permanent theatre at the Foire St-Laurent, built in 1721. The actors still parade

dramatists, Le Sage, better known now for his novels *Gil Blas* and *Le Diable boiteux*, should have quarrelled with them after the production of his finest play, *Turcaret*. Like Marivaux in the early part of his career, Le Sage was deeply indebted to the Spanish theatre. But *Turcaret*, a bitter comedy on the subject of *parvenu* financiers and the iniquities of the tax system, was in the old tradition of French comedy. It shows what its author might have done for the established theatre had he not chosen to waste his talents on ephemeral productions for the unlicensed theatre companies of the Paris fairgrounds. *Ill. 154* These *forains*, as they were called, encouraged by dramatists of the calibre of Le Sage, flourished well enough to build themselves

Ill. 155   permanent theatres, to become part-founders with the Italians of the Opéra-Comique, and to provide one of the outstanding theatrical attractions of Paris in the nineteenth century.

Meanwhile, audiences at the Comédie-Française, deprived of Le Sage and neglectful of Marivaux, were enjoying the tearful comedies – *comédies larmoyantes* – of Nivelle de la Chaussée, which, with the moral *drames* of Denis Diderot, mark the main contribution of the eighteenth century to the literary history of the French theatre. Both are the logical outcome of the influx into the playhouses of a middle-class audience demanding strong emotional situations in a recognizably contemporary setting. The doctrine of the equality of man brought the tragic hero from the palace into the parlour, while the sensibility of an audience which included far more women than before enjoyed being touched to tears even at a comedy. It was the misfortune of France, as of other countries at this time, to have no dramatist capable of making great theatre out of the material to hand. Luckily there was no lack of good actors, playing in well-proportioned and well-equipped theatres which had not yet been demolished to make way for the enormous playhouses of the next century.

Before tragedy finally declined into *drame bourgeois* it enjoyed one
Ill. 159   last brief blaze of glory at the hands of that universal genius, Voltaire, who like Goethe devoted part of his time and energy to the theatre. He built several private playhouses, the best being that at Ferney, his last home, and he was himself a good amateur actor and a great promoter of theatrical activities. But even his earliest tragedies, which are classical in form and continue the illusion of greatness, show traces of the influence of Shakespeare, whom Voltaire was the first Frenchman to admire, though with reservations. His later plays are unashamedly *drames bourgeois* and even *comédies larmoyantes*. In them he mingled tragedy and comedy, and employed crowd scenes and spectacular effects in a way which completed the divorce of French tragedy from its seventeenth-century roots. The crowds and spectacles, however, served one good purpose. They led to the removal from the stage of the audience, who can still be seen encroaching on the acting area in the engraving of the first production

156 A scene from Voltaire's *Sémiramis* at the Comédie-Française in 1748, showing spectators seated on both sides of the stage

of *Sémiramis* in 1748, but who have been banished to the audi- *Ill. 156*
torium by the time of the revival in 1759. Three years later Garrick
was able to effect the same long overdue reform in London.

It is interesting to note, since Garrick's name has come up, that he
was the only English actor of his day to be admired on the Continent,
where he travelled extensively between 1763 and 1765. He was
particularly esteemed in France, where he had many friends, and
though he never appeared on the French – or indeed on any foreign
– stage, he gave several solo performances in private houses in Paris,
amazing the spectators by the mobility of his face, the expressiveness
of his gestures, and the enormous range of his voice. They were more
used to the traditional declamation and statuesque poses of their
own leading actors. If Garrick learned much from the French
theatre, and made use of his knowledge at Drury Lane, in return
his natural style of acting may have influenced some of the French
actors who watched his performances, particularly the great Lekain,
friend and protégé of Voltaire.

Voltaire was indeed singularly fortunate in his interpreters. Among the earliest were La Noue, a fine provincial actor and playwright whom Voltaire introduced into the company of the Comédie-Française, and the lovely and ill-fated Adrienne Lecouvreur, who died in his arms and whose hurried and unsanctified burial moved him to make a bitter attack upon the Church. Actors were still 'rogues and vagabonds' in France, and suffered the penalty of excommunication. Even Molière was buried by night and probably in unconsecrated ground. For Voltaire the plight of Adrienne Lecouvreur, whose short but glorious career was later made the subject of a play which provided an enviable part for many good actresses, was rendered even more poignant by contrast with the funeral of the English actress Anne Oldfield, who was buried near Congreve in Westminster Abbey in the same year, 1730, and whom Voltaire much admired, saying she was the only actress in London whose speech he could follow without difficulty.

Ill. 157

157 Adrienne Lecouvreur (1692–1730), who appeared in some of the early plays of Voltaire, seen here as Cornélie, the wife of Pompey, in a revival of Corneille's *La Mort de Pompée, c.* 1725. She carries an urn containing the ashes of her murdered husband

158 Henri-Louis Lekain (1729–78), a great French tragic actor who was often compared to Garrick, his English contemporary, seen here as Genghis Khan in Voltaire's *L'Orphelin de la Chine*

Just as Voltaire had discovered and brought to Paris La Noue, the interpreter of his Mahomet in 1741, so he discovered and trained the great actor Lekain, taking him at the age of nineteen into his own *Ill. 158* house and making a room there into a theatre for him. With an amateur company composed of Voltaire's friends and relations, Lekain acted there for six months. This provided him with an excellent introduction to the stage, and before Voltaire left Paris in 1750 he was able to see his protégé make his début at the Comédie-Française as Titus in his benefactor's *Rome sauvée*. Although he was small and hard-featured, and had a harsh voice, Lekain had more than a spark of genius, and his career was one of unbroken triumph. He made his last appearance also in one of Voltaire's plays, a revival of *Adélaïde du Guesclin*, in 1778. Emerging into the night air after the performance, he caught a chill and died just as Voltaire was returning to Paris after his long exile, to die in the same year.

157

Apart from his excellence as an actor Lekain is important in the history of the French theatre as the first man to attempt some historical accuracy in stage costume. He discarded the plumed headdress and long cloak of the tragic hero for a simpler classic garb, and dressed his minor actors in costumes suitable to the period of the play. In his reforms he was strongly supported by his leading lady, Mlle Clairon, who also acted in many of Voltaire's plays. In his *L'Orphelin de la Chine* in 1755 she discarded her panniers for a simple flowing

Ill. 160

159 (*left*) The 'apotheosis' of Voltaire on
30 March 1778, at the Comédie-Française, after
the sixth performance of his *Irène*. Voltaire
himself was present in the top box, stage right

160 (*above*) A scene from Voltaire's *L'Orphelin
de la Chine* (1755) with Lekain as Genghis Khan
and Mlle Clairon as Idamé, seen pleading for
the life of her child

robe with loose sleeves. This may not have been particularly Chinese,
but it was a step in the right direction. And as Roxane in a revival of
Racine's *Bajazet* at about the same time she appeared in a close
approximation to a Turkish lady's dress.

While Lekain and Mlle Clairon were keeping alive the tradition
of French acting inherited directly from Molière, the Comédie-
Italienne, now Italian in name only, was staging the plays specially
written for it in French by the Italian dramatist Goldoni, who had

settled in Paris in 1761. His earlier efforts in Venice to revive the moribund and verbally indecent *commedia dell'arte* by providing its actors with written texts had for a time met with success. An interesting mingling of the old and new styles is apparent in his *Servant of Two Masters*, a play which has proved popular in translation in Russia, in England, and in the United States in a production by Max Reinhardt. His most successful period was from 1748 to 1753, when his plays were given at the Teatro Sant'Angelo in Venice by a company under Medebac, for which he wrote such masterpieces as *La vedova scaltra*, *Il bugiardo*, and, perhaps his best-known work, *La locandiera* (of which there are at least seven English translations). The heroine, Mirandolina, the mistress of the inn, later proved a popular part with many actresses, particularly Duse.

Unfortunately, Goldoni left Medebac to write for Vendramin's company at the Teatro San Luca (now the Teatro Goldoni), which was larger and really more suited to spectacular shows than to his intimate comedies. Although he had to contend not only with the attacks of his rival Gozzi but also with those of a mediocre playwright named Pietro Chiari, he remained with Vendramin for eight years, writing during this time some of his best plays, including *I rusteghi* and *Le donne curiose*, both used later for the libretti of operas by Wolf-Ferrari. Of his French plays the first, and most successful, was *Le Bourru bienfaisant*. He also left an excellent volume of memoirs, written in French, which is useful for the theatrical history of his time.

French drama was to have one last brilliant phase before the upheavals of the Revolution with two fine plays by Beaumarchais, *Le Barbier de Séville* and *Le Mariage de Figaro*. These are too often thought of merely as the source of Rossini's and Mozart's operas. But in their original form they are highly entertaining comedies, and continue the tradition of Spanish influence on French dramatic literature which began with *Le Cid*. Between them they sum up the life and character of their extraordinary and many-sided author. He was himself the precocious page Cherubin, the handsome Almaviva (he was three times married), and above all the resourceful Figaro, jack-of-all-trades, often in trouble but always landing on his feet, clever and unscrupulous. Politically both plays were considered

Ills. 161, 163

dangerous, and it took much time and energy to get them past the censor. *Le Barbier de Séville* was acted in 1775 to amuse an audience which still felt secure from the Revolution it predicted, but by 1784, when *Le Mariage de Figaro* was first produced, the public was beginning to recognize the dangers which lay before it. The criticisms of Figaro, older and wiser, are no longer directed against an individual, but against society as a whole.

Both these plays were produced at the Comédie-Française, which had now left the theatre it had occupied since 1689 for a new building on the present site of the Odéon. Its leading actors were Préville, who *Ill. 162* had succeeded Raisin, known as 'le petit Molière', as chief comedian, playing Figaro in *Le Barbier de Séville*, and Molé, the Almaviva of *Ill. 161* that play and of its sequel, *Le Mariage de Figaro*, in which Louise *Ill. 163* Contat played Suzanne. Molé, who was outstanding in comedy, was by a curious irony destined to be the first French Hamlet, in an adaptation by Ducis. He was also the teacher and later the close friend of the leading actor Talma, who was to guide the Comédie- *Ill. 170* Française through the ravages of the French Revolution, and having weathered the storm, to see it established more firmly than ever under the aegis of Napoleon.

In Italy, apart from Goldoni and Gozzi, the only playwright worthy of note is Alfieri, the devoted lover of the Countess of Albany, wife of the Young Pretender. His two best tragedies, by common consent, are *Saul* and *Mirra*, both on Biblical subjects. The other seventeen are on classical themes. All are marked by extreme severity of style and austerity of form, and observe strictly the three unities already discarded in France. Alfieri also wrote some comedies, now forgotten, which may however be due for reappraisal, and, like Goldoni, an interesting volume of memoirs.

For the rest, Italy was given over to opera, and the dramatic genius of Apostolo Zeno and Metastasio was employed in the writing of libretti. Some of these were set by many different composers and produced with sumptuous décors by the best stage-designers of the day, inheritors of the traditions of the Bibienas, Burnacini, and Juvarra. Among them one of the most interesting was Jean-Nicolas Servandony, who studied and worked in Italy, and on one occasion *Ill. 164*

161 (*above*) A contemporary sketch of a scene from *Le Barbier de Séville* (1775) by Pierre-Augustin Caron de Beaumarchais (1732–99), with Molé as Almaviva and Mlle Doligny as Rosine

162 (*left*) The actor Préville (1721–99) in the striped costume of Mezzetin, a portrait by Carle Van Loo

163 (*above right*) Beaumarchais's *Le Mariage de Figaro* (1784), again with Molé as Almaviva, and with Mlle Contat as Suzanne

164 (*right*) A stage-set in diagonal perspective by Jean-Nicolas Servandony (1695–1766), its severe architectural solidity in direct contrast to the lightness and elegance of the late baroque and rococo styles (*Ill. 165*), and showing very clearly the influence of the Bibienas' *scena d'angolo* (see *Ill. 52*)

was invited to work in Portugal, which had also succumbed to the craze for opera. Going thence to France, he took over the Salle des Machines in the Tuileries, where his work in its turn influenced the designers of Italy and Germany. The rococo style which had evolved from the debasement of the baroque was typified in France by *Ill. 165* Boquet, whose designs for costumes and scenery, both for opera and for Court entertainments, had decisive repercussions on the legitimate stage. The supremacy in stage design of Italy, whose artists had once been found in the theatres of every European town, had now passed to France. Even England, who by reason of her isolation, as well as her temperament, had escaped the influence of the baroque style, was indebted to a Frenchman, Garrick's designer de Loutherbourg, for the scenic style of the London playhouses at the end of the eighteenth century.

165 A graceful stage-set in rococo style by Louis-René Boquet (*fl.* 1760–82), who worked both for the Opéra and for the Court entertainments at Versailles and Fontainebleau

CHAPTER NINE

The Early Nineteenth-century Theatre

The mid-eighteenth century, which saw the emergence of a national theatre in Germany, and a great consolidation of theatrical enter-prises in other European countries, saw also the permanent establish-ment of the theatre on the eastern side of the North American continent. Plays in Spanish had been given on the west coast as early as 1538, and again in 1598. Plays in French were seen in Quebec in the early seventeenth century. But these were isolated incidents which produced no lasting results. It was the visiting actors from England, landing first in Virginia, who laid the foundations of the American theatre, and along English lines that it developed. The early manifestations were sporadic. A playhouse was built in Williamsburg *c.* 1716 for a company headed by Charles and Mary Stagg; during the 1730s a company at Charleston's first Dock Street Theatre was producing such London successes as *The Orphan* and *The Recruiting Officer*; and in 1749 'the Virginia Company of Comedians', led by Thomas Kean and Walter Murray, was in Philadelphia. These three towns were the main centres of theatrical activity, though most visiting actors managed a trip to New York, where in 1750 Kean and Murray opened a temporary playhouse on Nassau Street with a repertory which included *Love for Love, The Beaux' Stratagem*, and *Richard III*, the last probably in Colley Cibber's version. In 1753 a second theatre on Nassau Street housed a company which Lewis Hallam had brought direct from London. The excel-lence of its acting and its varied repertory gave a great impetus to the development of the theatre in the New World, though it still had to contend with the innate Puritanism bequeathed by the early settlers, as well as bad roads and inadequate accommodation. Nevertheless, it succeeded in establishing a foothold with the building of such theatres as the Southwark in Philadelphia and the John Street in New York, which resembled Potter's Little Theatre in London's

Haymarket. After Hallam's death in Jamaica in 1756 his widow had married a rival manager, David Douglass, and it was their combined troupe which, with Hallam's son Lewis as its leading man, opened the John Street Theatre in 1767 with *The Beaux' Stratagem*. Billed as The American Company, they also appeared at the second Dock Street *Ill. 166* Theatre in Charleston, and toured with success until the outbreak of war drove them to the West Indies. But even during hostilities the infant theatre managed to survive. The John Street building was used for performances by British Officers, among them the famous spy Major John André, who both acted and painted scenery. Meanwhile, far away in Valley Forge, Addison's *Cato* was being performed in the opposing camp before George Washington himself.

After they gained their independence several of the new American states tried to prohibit acting on the grounds that it roused undesirable passions. But the professional actors crept back, and in 1785 The American Company, now under the management of the younger Hallam and the Irish actor John Henry, came back to New York and gave regular seasons at the John Street Theatre. Here they produced in 1787 the first American comedy, Royall Tyler's *The Contrast*. Like *Othello*, this had to be disguised as a 'Moral Lecture' before it could be acted in Boston, the author's birthplace, where prejudice against the theatre was to remain strong for many years. John Henry, who had added to his company the fine English actor John Hodgkinson, also produced in 1789 *The Father; or, American Shandyism*, by William Dunlap, the first outstanding American-born 'man of the theatre' and a dominating force on the American stage from 1790 to 1810. He had been sent to London to study art, but turned to the theatre, and took advantage of his stay in London to study the work of the leading actors of the day. He then returned to America to take over the management of the John Street Theatre, and strengthened *Ill. 167* the company in 1796 by taking on the first Joseph Jefferson, founder of a famous American theatrical family. Two years later Dunlap, with Hodgkinson, opened the Park Theatre in New York. One of the first plays to be performed was *André*, based on the life of the play-acting spy of the War of Independence, which thus ranks as the first native play on American material. Hodgkinson played André,

166

167 William Dunlap's painting of the Screen Scene from an American production of Sheridan's *The School for Scandal*, probably at the Park Theatre, New York, c. 1802, with Joseph Jefferson the First as Sir Peter Teazle (*cf. Ill. 125*) ▶

166 The restored eighteenth-century Dock Street Theatre in Charleston, South
Carolina, showing the influence of the contemporary English theatre (*Ill. 117*)

and in the company was Thomas Cooper, a young actor newly arrived from London. He was later to succeed Dunlap in the management of the Park Theatre, and to prove a vital element in the development of the theatre in the United States.

The success of the John Street Theatre, which was several times visited by George Washington, and of the Park Theatre, had for a time assured the supremacy of New York in theatrical matters. But in 1794 Thomas Wignell, who had been the leading comedian of The American Company, left and went to Philadelphia. Here he opened the handsome and elegant Chestnut Street Theatre, built from the plans of the Theatre Royal at Bath, and incidentally the first theatre in America to be lit by gas, even before London's Drury Lane. With an excellent company which included Wallack and his wife, from London, and three of the Jefferson family, Wignell established a tradition of light-comedy acting which caused his theatre to be nicknamed 'Old Drury'. It held the monopoly of acting in Philadelphia until the opening in 1811 of the Walnut Street Theatre, which is still in use and is now the oldest theatre in the United States. The rivalry between the two theatres, and the disastrous policy of

Ill. 168

168 (*left*) The Chestnut Street
Theatre, Philadelphia, built in 1793
to house the company brought
from London by Thomas Wignell
(1753–1803), whose members soon
gave it an enviable reputation

169 (*right*) Helena Modjeska
(1840–1909), a Polish actress who
appeared with great success in
the United States and London,
particularly in Shakespeare, seen
here as Ophelia in the Mad Scene
in 1889

importing expensive stars from Europe, led eventually to bankruptcy, and the supremacy in theatrical matters again passed to New
York, where it still remains, though threatened by the recent
establishment of theatres all over the country.

The time was coming when the United States would produce its
own outstanding actors – dramatists came on the scene much later.
But for some time to come the chief diversion of American audiences
would be the meteoric appearances of visiting stars, who were very
ready to take advantage of this fresh source of adulation and income.
After Edmund Kean, Cooke and Macready from London came
Rachel and Fechter from Paris, Janauschek from Prague, Modjeska   *Ill. 169*
from Warsaw, Ristori and Salvini from Italy. They appeared
mainly in a repertory of well-known older plays, for Europe had
little of value that was new to send. But the American audiences in
the making were primarily interested in acting, and in that respect
they were well served.

In Europe the early years of the nineteenth century were not
propitious for theatrical experiments. One might have expected great
things of France, where the Revolution had swept away a monopoly

169

170 (*right*) François-Joseph Talma (1763–1826) as Nero in Racine's *Britannicus* (first produced in 1661). He was the first French actor to play Roman parts in a toga, instead of in contemporary dress or the ubiquitous kilt

171 (*far right*) The Comédie-Française, as it was in 1808. For a theatre of the same date in London, see Drury Lane (*Ill. 174*)

that in England was to endure until 1843. But the stultifying effects of revolutionary excesses, followed by the rapid establishment of the Consulate and the Empire, left little time or energy for innovation.

Ill. 170 Napoleon, who much admired the acting of Talma, found time to arrange for the re-establishment of the dispersed company of the

Ill. 171 Comédie-Française. He settled it on the site which it still occupies and drew up for it the constitution under which it still functions. But he did not allow his dramatists the freedom accorded to Molière by Louis XIV, and the serious theatre suffered under his rule. It was the lighter forms of entertainment that flourished – the operetta, the vaudeville, and the melodramas of Pixérécourt, who wrote, as he himself said, for those who could not read. His plays, with their mingled violence and sentimentality, their elaborate settings and stage effects and their scenes of rapid action underlined by suitable

music, made expert use of a small number of well-worn themes, in which, after the pleasurable excitements of vice, virtue triumphed. They delighted the illiterate, uncritical new audiences that crowded the popular theatres, and soon found their way into England. In 1802 Thomas Holcroft put on at Covent Garden a translation of *Coelina, ou l'enfant de mystère* as *A Tale of Mystery* – the first English play to be labelled a 'Melodrama'. No mention of Pixérécourt was made, and later many of his plays were plagiarized in this way, without acknowledgement, the law of copyright being not yet in force.

Both Covent Garden and Drury Lane succumbed to the mania for melodrama. The vast size of both playhouses tempted their managers to retain a hold on the restless audiences by all the spectacular devices the stage carpenters and machinists could devise. There was no lack of fires, floods and earthquakes, and many plays employed real

Ill. 174

172 (*left*) Mrs Siddons (*née* Sarah Kemble, 1755–1831), one of England's most famous tragic actresses and the outstanding member of a great theatrical family; a sketch made of her in youth by George Romney

173 (*below left*) John Philip Kemble (1757–1823), the eldest son of the Kemble family and brother of Mrs Siddons. A stately, formal actor, at his best in tragic and heavily dramatic parts, he is seen here as Shakespeare's Coriolanus, in a portrait by Sir Thomas Lawrence

174 Drury Lane Theatre in 1808, after the rebuilding by Sheridan in 1794. Mrs Siddons called it 'a wilderness of a place', and the immense auditorium led the actors to enlarge their gestures and amplify their voices to the detriment of their technique

Ills. 172, 173

animals – dogs, horses, even elephants. The serious dramatists were unable to compete with such distractions, and it was on inferior new plays of good craftsmanship that the fine actors of the day wasted their powers. Both John Philip Kemble and his sister Sarah Siddons appeared in adaptations of Kotzebue, Kemble as Rolla in *Pizarro* (by no less a person than Sheridan) and Mrs Siddons as Mrs Haller, the erring wife in *The Stranger*, one of her favourite parts. Yet both could rise to the heights of Shakespearian tragedy when they wished. Kemble's Hamlet and Mrs Siddons's Lady Macbeth were highly thought of. But tragedy did not fill the playhouses, and neither of them had much gift for comedy. In this they were outshone by their youngest brother Charles. Stephen, the second brother, who was so fat that he could play Falstaff without padding, was neither a good

175 An 'all-purpose' setting for historical plays designed by William Capon (1757–1827). Capon had designed many sets both for Covent Garden and for Drury Lane, but they were lost when the theatres were destroyed by fire in 1808 and 1809. This set was for the new Covent Garden, opened by Kemble in 1809

actor nor a good manager. Charles, however, excelled in fine-gentleman parts – Romeo, Orlando, Mercutio, Mirabell, Charles Surface, and Young Absolute. All these, it will be noted, were revivals, for nothing new of permanent value was being written. In the same way Charles's daughter Fanny, one of the leading actresses of her day, made her reputation both in England and in the United States, where she married and retired from the stage for a time, in such parts as Juliet, Portia, Beatrice, Lady Teazle, and Belvidera in *Venice Preserved*.

As managers and actors John Philip and Charles Kemble were much concerned with the provision of costumes and scenery for their theatres. By the 1820s both Covent Garden and Drury Lane, in common with theatres everywhere, had replaced their candles and oil-lamps by gas lighting, an innovation which was to have far-reaching results. The main attractions of gas were the increase in illumination and the fact that the intensity of light could be controlled at will. The wavering flames – which unfortunately did little to diminish the risk of fire – still imparted, though more brilliantly, the shimmering effect which was one of the chief attractions of candlelight. It was the mysterious atmosphere this gave which was most bitterly regretted when, towards the end of the nineteenth century, gas was superseded by the hard, steady glare of electricity.

One of the designers employed by the Kembles was William Capon. His work shows the influence of de Loutherbourg, but his *Ills. 175, 120* passion for 'authenticity' led him to design a number of neo-gothic settings 'suitable for Shakespeare's plays' which dominated scene-design during the next half-century. The great names in scene-painting during this time were Clarkson Stanfield and the Grieve family. The latter's ascendency lasted through three generations. John, the founder of the family, worked for Kemble. The moonlit scenes of his son William were particularly admired, and he was the first scene-designer to be called for by the audience. John's grandson Thomas, who worked for Charles Kean, was noted for the brilliance of his sets and the artistic unity of their composition.

Together with a desire for accuracy in settings went that for historically correct costumes. It was for Charles Kemble's production

176 (*left*) George Frederick
Cooke (1756–1812) as
Richard III, wearing the
plumed hat and high boots
of the Restoration tragic hero
combined with Elizabethan
doublet and hose, sur-
mounted by a short
ermine-trimmed cloak

178 (*right*) Edmund Kean ▶
(1787/90–1833) as Othello,
after a painting by Lambert.
Kean first played this part in
London at Drury Lane in
1814, and thereafter many
times

177 An historically accurate
costume designed by James
Robinson Planché
(1796–1880) for a production
of *King John* by Charles
Kemble at Covent Garden
in 1824

of *King John* at Covent Garden in 1824 that the playwright Planché,
who was also a noted antiquarian, designed costumes which were
Ill. 177 based on sound scholarship and a thorough knowledge of heraldry,
and so set a precedent which was followed by Charles Kean, son of
the Kembles' only rival, Edmund.

Ill. 178 Edmund Kean, a foundling child who grew up in the theatre, was
a rough, untutored genius, at his best in strong villainous parts like
Richard III, Iago, or Marlowe's Jew of Malta, Barabas. As Shakespeare's Jew, Shylock, he electrified the audience at Drury Lane by
jettisoning the red hair and beard which even Macklin had not dared
to discard, and making the character a swarthy fiend with a butcher's
knife in his grasp and blood-lust in his eyes. Kean, who was a heavy
drinker, was an unbalanced and unpredictable actor, but he was
perhaps needed in a theatre dominated by the 'noble' John Philip
Kemble and the 'gentlemanly' Charles. George Frederick Cooke,
who might have helped to redress the balance, was as alcoholic and
unreliable as Kean, and spent most of his life in the English provinces.
Ill. 176 Yet when he played Richard III at Covent Garden he gave such a
remarkable performance that Kemble swore never to play the part
again; and when he made his first appearance in the United States
at the Park Theatre, New York, he was given a tumultuous welcome.
But the audiences who had acclaimed him as the greatest tragic actor
they had ever seen fell away when his habitual intemperance and
unreliability returned. After a disastrous tour he returned to die in
New York, where Kean, who thought highly of his capabilities,
erected a monument to him.

Kean's son Charles, who also toured extensively in the United
States, was a quieter, more polished player, very unlike his tempera-
mental father. In the days of affluence which followed Kean's
triumphant début at Drury Lane in 1814 Charles had been sent to
Eton in the hope of keeping him off the stage. But when the father's
behaviour grew too scandalous to bear, Drury Lane dismissed him
and Charles took his place both as actor and as breadwinner for the
family. Father and son acted together only once, at Covent Garden,
as Othello and Iago. Edmund collapsed on stage and died shortly
afterwards. With none of his father's genius, Charles was nevertheless

178

a good reliable actor and an excellent manager, who had a most salutary influence on the theatre of his time. With his wife, Ellen Tree, who was also his leading lady, he led for many years a company which had its greatest successes at the Princess's Theatre from 1850 to 1859. Kean's productions of Shakespeare and adaptations of *Ill. 179* French drama – *The Corsican Brothers, Pauline, Louis XI* – were often *Ill. 196* attended by Queen Victoria. They were sumptuously staged, and benefited from Kean's attention to detail, from the harmony established between the various component parts of the play – the speech, music and scenery – and particularly from the handling of the crowd scenes in Shakespeare.

179 A setting for *Richard II* – 'the wilds of Gloucestershire' – in the production at the Princess's Theatre in 1857 by Charles Kean (1811–68), who himself played Richard, with John Ryder as Bolingbroke

By a curious link in theatre history, these productions by Charles Kean in London were to influence staging in Europe, where they were never seen. George, Duke of Saxe-Meiningen, had married a niece of Queen Victoria, and on his visits to London had had many chances of visiting the Princess's. He was passionately fond of the theatre and after the death of his first wife married morganatically the actress Ellen Franz. With her he established at his Court a company which became famous as the Meiningers. The Duke, ably assisted by the actor Ludwig Chronegk, directed the productions and *Ill. 180* designed the scenery and costumes with a high degree of historical accuracy. Applying Charles Kean's methods, he broke away from the formal grouping of leading actors common on the Continental stage at the time, and divided the crowd into groups, each with a leader, each player a character in his own right. By the use of steps and rostrums he also kept the action flowing continuously. When the Meiningers first went on tour in the 1870s they were widely acclaimed. Even in London their *Julius Caesar* and *Twelfth Night* were highly thought of, and their influence was later apparent in productions as far apart as Moscow and Paris. There was however one person in Germany whose influence on the early history of the Meiningers has been somewhat overlooked – Richard Wagner, who belongs properly to the history of opera, but who was also a great innovator in stage matters, particularly in lighting, designing and choreography. His vision of the 'complete work of art' must be taken into account in any survey of the nineteenth-century theatre in Europe.

Unfortunately, the German theatre, even after the country had recovered from the tragic aftermath of the Napoleonic Wars, remained faithful to melodrama and to the 'well-made' plays of France, and the only dramatist of note was Hebbel. Political supremacy and unification under the Hohenzollerns provided a poor soil for serious drama, which had to wait for a fertilizing influence from outside. Only in Vienna, where the genius of the young Grill-parzer was discovered and fostered by Schreyvogel, was there renewed vitality, and that was mainly in the domain of popular theatre. In 1788 Marinelli's Theater in der Leopoldstadt had acquired

180 A design of *c*. 1875 by George II, Duke of Saxe-Meiningen (1826–1914) for a scene in *Der Prinz von Homburg*, by Heinrich von Kleist (1777–1811), which formed part of the repertory of the Meininger company

a powerful rival in Mayer's Theater in der Josefstadt, and in 1801 Schickaneder, the librettist of Mozart's *Magic Flute*, opened the famous Theater an der Wien. This was the culminating point of his career as impresario, playwright and actor, during which he had appeared with equal success in *Hamlet*, folk-comedy and opera, and in the *Singspiele*, or ballad-operas, so popular with his royal patron Joseph II.

The day of the extempore farce was over, but a new type of popular play, the *Zauberstück*, took its place. This mixture of magic, farce and parody, which was akin to the English pantomime, had its roots far back in the baroque theatre. In the hands of three immensely productive writers, Gleich, Meisl and Bäuerle – this last the creator of the comic figure Staberl, popularized throughout Austria by the

Ill. 184   actor Karl Carl – it prepared the way for the great comedies of Raimund and Nestroy, who were to dominate the Viennese theatre for so long. Raimund, the leading comic actor of his time, served his apprenticeship in the popular theatre. He soon realized that his unique combination of wistful irony and delicately sentimental pathos needed specially written material, which he decided to provide for
Ill. 181   himself. This resulted in such plays as *Das Mädchen aus der Feenwelt* and *Der Alpenkönig und der Menschenfeind*. These are moral tales in which mortals learn from magic beings the basic truths of life, and in which spectacle, charade, transformation scenes, music and singing all receive new life from the genius of this typically Viennese playwright.

Raimund was the product of Romanticism and of the old order,
Ill. 184   which lasted longer in Austria than anywhere else. Nestroy, who succeeded, and destroyed, him, was a man of the new world whose dissatisfactions culminated in the revolutions of 1848. A facile writer, and a pilferer of plots, his bitter destructive satire often brought him into conflict with the authorities. But he bounced up again, dazzling his audiences with improvisation and superb character-acting. Though wittier than Raimund, he had less imagination and less heart. He excelled in parody, Wagner being one of his main targets. After him the phenomenon of the folk-theatre declined into Viennese operetta, which conquered the theatres of the world to the beat of waltz-time.

There was no dramatist in France to do for the serious theatre what Grillparzer did for Austria with his tragedies, of which *Der Traum ein*
Ill. 182   *Leben* echoed Calderón's *La vida es sueño*. The fervent apostles of Romanticism did their best to fill the gap with Victor Hugo's plays,
Ill. 183   particularly *Hernani* – which led to the stormiest first night the Comédie-Française had known for some time – and *Ruy Blas*. Both show the traditional influence of Spain. There were also the plays of the elder Dumas, and Alfred de Vigny's *Chatterton*, first-fruits of the English influence imported with Shakespeare, who was fully revealed to a French audience by the visit in 1827 of a company under Charles
Ill. 185   Kemble. His leading lady was Harriet Smithson, who soon after became the wife of Berlioz. The life of the Romantic theatre was

181 Ferdinand Raimund (1790–
1836) as the 'Aschenmann' in his
own play *Das Mädchen aus der
Feenwelt, oder der Bauer als
Millionär* (1826)

short. Dumas was primarily a novelist, Hugo and de Vigny were poets. The charming comedies of Alfred de Musset were not written for the stage, and had to be rediscovered in Russia by a young French actress and brought back to Paris twenty years later. The true theatre of the time was still to be found in vaudeville and melodrama, and in the works of the prolific Scribe, who during all the excesses of Romanticism continued imperturbably to turn out his 'well-made' plays, which set a pattern for dramatists everywhere. Unlike the Romantics, who made high tragedy of everyday happenings, Scribe excelled in bringing great historical events down to the level of the back parlour. But his technique was superb. His closely-knit plots and orderly tying-off of loose ends appealed to the logical French mind, and provided a welcome relief to an audience which had been introduced somewhat hurriedly to the splendid irrelevancies of Shakespeare and his imitators.

182 (*above left*) A scene from the tragedy *Der Traum ein Leben*, by the Austrian Franz Grillparzer, at the Vienna Burgtheater in 1834

184 (*above*) Viennese popular theatre: Nestroy's *Lumpazivagabundus*, 1833, with the actor-manager Karl Carl centre stage, and Nestroy himself on his right

183 (*left*) The uproar in the auditorium of the Comédie-Française during the first night of *Hernani* (25 February 1830) by Victor Hugo

185 (*right*) Charles Kemble and Harriet Smithson as Romeo and Juliet in a season of Shakespeare at the Odéon, Paris, in 1827, a revelation to the young Romantics

CHAPTER TEN

The Later Nineteenth-century Theatre

Between 1830 and 1880 the theatre everywhere expanded rapidly. New buildings were put up to accommodate increasingly large but undiscriminating audiences, more people found work on or behind the stage, prolific dramatists turned out hundreds of ephemeral plays which owed more to the splendour of their settings and the excellence of the actors than to plot or dialogue. In France the Comédie-Française, though still the leading theatre of Paris, found its pre-eminence challenged by the new theatres, of which the Odéon was the most important. Founded by Picard, a playwright whose musical comedy, *La petite Ville*, went to Germany as *Die lustige Witwe* and so to England as *The Merry Widow*, it was taken over in 1829 by Harel. It then deserted musical plays for a classical and contemporary repertory which gave it the position it still holds as France's second theatre. There, and in theatres like the Porte-Saint-Martin and the

Ill. 186   Renaissance, great reputations were made by such actors as Frédérick, the first Ruy Blas, famous also for his portrayal of Macaire; Deburau, the beloved Pierrot and pantomimist of the Funambules on the Boulevard du Temple, whose many theatres were swept away by Haussmann in 1862; and Marie Dorval, the heroine of many romantic dramas, who was already famous when she went to the Comédie-Française to play Kitty Bell in *Chatterton*. Even the leading members of the Comédie-Française itself were often absent on tour. Rachel, whose appearance in Racine's plays had revived the glories of

Ill. 187   French classical drama after a period of neglect, visited England in 1841 and the United States in 1855. During her absence the Comédie-Française was glad for the first time in its career to take over plays which had been successful elsewhere. Among them was Augier's best-known work, *Le Gendre de M. Poirier*. Augier, who also wrote *Les Lionnes pauvres* and *Le Fils de Giboyeur*, was one of the dramatists of the new era which began with the Revolution of 1848, and a

186

187 The great tragic actress Rachel (1820–58) at Covent Garden in 1841, making ▶
her farewell appearance as Camille in Corneille's *Horace*. Note the stage boxes

186 The actor Antoine-Louis-Prosper Lemaître (1800–76), known as Frédérick (*centre*), with the novelist-playwright Honoré de Balzac (*left*) and the Romantic Théophile Gautier (*right*), painted by Gautier himself in 1840

greater realist than most of his contemporaries, of whom the best known is the younger Dumas.

Dumas's plays of social criticism, *Le Demi-monde*, *Le Fils naturel*, and *Un Père prodigue* (the last two written from bitter experience as the illegitimate son of the effervescent elder Dumas), were overshadowed by the success of his first play, *La Dame aux camélias*. This was a sentimental portrayal of the courtesan with a heart of gold, Marguerite Gautier, which has provided a splendid vehicle for leading ladies ever since its first production. The hero, the young Armand Duval, was first acted by Charles Fechter, the son of an English mother and a French father of German extraction, who was equally at home everywhere. After a successful career in Paris he went to London and then to the United States, where he remained until his death. Although his English accent was never good, he had enough fluency and self-confidence to give a good account of himself as Ruy Blas in a translation of Hugo's play. It was however his revolutionary *Ill. 189* Hamlet in 1861 which first brought him into prominence, and led to his appearing at the Lyceum in London in melodrama, under his own

management. The Lyceum, like the Olympic and the Princess's, had become important in the theatrical life of London after the Theatres Act of 1843 had broken the monopoly of Drury Lane and Covent Garden. This had been a less epoch-making event than might have been supposed. The unlicensed theatres had for a long time been evading the law by inserting half a dozen songs into any play, even one by Shakespeare, and calling it a burletta. The licensed theatres too had been giving their patrons much the same fare as the unlicensed. Macready, a powerful actor who after Kemble's retirement was Edmund Kean's only rival in tragedy, had endeavoured to keep up the standard at both houses with such new plays as *Virginius*, by Sheridan Knowles; *Werner*, by Lord Byron, who was for a short *Ill. 190* time on the Committee of Drury Lane; and *The Lady of Lyons*, by the novelist Bulwer Lytton. But both Patent theatres put on melodramas like *The Dog of Montargis*, with its canine star, and *Hyder Ali; or, the Lions of Mysore*, which called for an entire menagerie of animal performers; and both did spectacular pantomimes annually at *Ill. 188* Christmas.

188 Grimaldi's Game of Leapfrog. Joseph Grimaldi as the Clown in *Harlequin Padmanada, or the Golden Fish*, a pantomime produced at Covent Garden at Christmas 1811. The frog, played by an actor in a frogskin, later appeared in an opera-hat and other fashionable accessories

189

Ill. 191
The one person who made a laudable attempt to turn the abolition of the monopoly to good account was Samuel Phelps. He had already made a name for himself as a tragedian on the York circuit when Macready engaged him to play Othello at Covent Garden. In 1843 he took over Sadler's Wells Theatre, and before he finally retired in 1862 he had staged nearly all Shakespeare's plays, some of them virtually unknown to his audiences. *Pericles*, for instance, had not been performed since the Restoration period. With Mrs Warner as his leading lady, Phelps appeared in most of the productions himself. Though he was at his best in such parts as Lear and Macbeth, he also made an excellent Bottom. In his well-run company he trained many young actors who were proud to say in later life that they had played with Phelps at the Wells.

Before appearing at Covent Garden Phelps had been seen briefly at the Haymarket, which continued to profit by the summer licence

189 (*far left*) Charles Fechter (1825–79) as Hamlet, at the Princess's Theatre, London, 1861

190 (*centre*) William Macready (1793–1873) as Werner in the play of that name by Lord Byron, with Mrs Faucit as his wife Josephine

191 (*left*) Samuel Phelps (1804–78) as Cardinal Wolsey in Shakespeare's *Henry VIII*, a painting by the actor Johnston Forbes-Robertson

obtained for it by Foote. It had been rebuilt on its present site in 1821, and was the last London theatre to be lit by candles, gas being installed only in 1843. In the remodelling it underwent then it lost those other relics of earlier days, the forestage and the proscenium doors. Its manager at this time was Ben Webster, member of a large and far-flung theatrical family, who in his youth had danced as Harlequin and Pantaloon in pantomime before turning to low comedy. He was excellent as John Peerybingle in his own adaptation of *The Cricket on the Hearth* – both Dickens and Scott provided adaptors with unlimited material for stage plays – but his best part was Triplet in *Masks and Faces*, by Tom Taylor, a play based on the life of Peg Woffington.

Webster had for a time been a member of Mme Vestris's company at the Olympic. Fresh from a triumphant career in Paris, this excellent actress, grand-daughter of the engraver Bartolozzi and deserted wife of the ballet-dancer Armand Vestris, delighted London audiences in the sparkling extravaganzas of Planché. She married as her second *Ill. 193* husband the light comedian Charles Mathews, son of the Mathews best remembered for his protean one-man entertainments *Mr Mathews at Home* and *The Actor of All Work*, in which he played all the parts himself. Together Mme Vestris and her husband went to Covent Garden, but their management was not a success. They fared better at the Lyceum, where for Planché's extravaganza *The Island of Jewels* the scene-painter Beverley designed the first transparency seen in London. Mme Vestris, who ruled her company with a stern hand, was an excellent manager and instituted many reforms, following the example of Charles Kean in historical costuming and the use of real properties. She is also believed to have been the first manager in *Ill. 192* London to employ the box-set (three walls with practicable doors and windows and a ceiling cloth over) instead of a backcloth with wings and sky borders.

One of the plays produced by Mme Vestris at Covent Garden during her tenancy was a comedy of contemporary life, *London Assurance*, in which Mathews made a great success as Dazzle. It was the first play of a young actor, Lee Morton, who under his real name of Boucicault became famous as actor and playwright in London and New York, dividing his time equally between them. He was a prolific author, being credited with one hundred and thirty plays. Many of them were adaptations from the French, among them *The* *Ill. 196* *Corsican Brothers* (which the equally prolific H. J. Byron burlesqued as *The Corsican 'Bothers'; or, the Troublesome Twins*), but his best work was done in his Irish dramas, *The Colleen Bawn*, *Arrah-na-Pogue* and *The Shaughraun*. In all of these his wife, Agnes Robertson, though a Scotswoman, played the heroines with great success. She was also, understandably, excellent as Jeanie Deans in her husband's dramatization of Scott's *The Heart of Midlothian*.

Webster had been succeeded at the Haymarket in 1853 by John Buckstone, another good low comedian (it was tragedians who were in short supply at this time). He already had a good reputation, having appeared in many of his own plays, of which the most successful were *Luke the Labourer* and *The Green Bushes*. The latter

192 A scene from *The Conquering Game*, by William Bernard, a one-act comedy produced at the Olympic Theatre in 1832 by Mme Vestris, with herself and her husband in the chief parts

193 (*below*) Mme Vestris (*née* Lucy Eliza Bartolozzi, 1797–1856), with her second husband Charles Mathews the younger (1803–78) in *Mr and Mrs Mathews at Home*

194 Edwin Booth (1833–93),
America's first outstanding native-
born actor, as Richelieu in Bulwer
Lytton's play of that name (first
produced in London in 1839),
at the Haymarket, London, in 1861

provided the mime-player Mme Céleste with one of her best parts.
At the Haymarket Buckstone gathered round him an excellent
company, and had an unbroken run of success. It was said that the
mere sound of his voice offstage was enough to set the audience
laughing. He loved the Haymarket so much that his ghost still
haunts it. During his tenancy a significant event took place, nothing
Ill. 194 less than the appearance in 1861 of Edwin Booth, the first actor from
the United States to win a European reputation. He appeared with
great success as Shylock, Richelieu and Sir Giles Overreach.

This, with Boucicault's career in New York, serves to show the
advance made by the American theatre in the preceding fifty years.
Before the end of the eighteenth century the theatre had established
itself even in puritanical Boston, where a Haymarket Theatre
opened in 1796. But New York still held the lead in theatrical life,
particularly after the rebuilding of the Park Theatre in 1820. The
elder Mathews appeared there, as did Junius Brutus Booth, Edwin's
father, after a successful career in London. But the Park's supremacy
was soon challenged within its own city when the Chatham opened

195 The American actress Charlotte Cushman (1816–76) as Romeo with Ada Swanborough as Juliet, at the Haymarket Theatre, London, 1855. Tall and plain, with a gruff voice, she had a hard struggle before her immense talent won her public esteem

196 (*below*) The duel scene in Dion Boucicault's famous melo-drama *The Corsican Brothers* at the Princess's Theatre, 1852, with Charles Kean as the dying Louis dei Franchi. He also played Louis's twin, Fabien, who avenges Louis's death

in 1824, followed by the Lafayette, and by the vast Bowery, which was burnt down and rebuilt four times before it finally closed in 1878. It was at the Bowery that the first outstanding American actress, Charlotte Cushman, who had something of the regal quality of Sarah Siddons, made her appearance in her most successful role, Lady Macbeth. She was also much admired as Queen Katharine in *Henry VIII*, and as Meg Merrilees in *Guy Mannering*. She was fond of appearing in men's parts, and played Wolsey and Claude Melnotte,

Ill. 195 as well as Romeo and Hamlet to the Juliet and Ophelia of her beautiful younger sister Susan.

The first outstanding American actor to be associated with the
Ill. 197 Bowery was Edwin Forrest. This fine tragedian was unfortunately bitterly jealous of Macready, whom he blamed for the failure of his second visit to London in 1845. When Macready again visited New York, Forrest's recriminations led to the Astor Place riots in which twenty-two people were killed. Macready himself had to be smuggled out of the town and put aboard a ship for England.

During the 1830s and 1840s the number of theatres in New York increased rapidly. They were mainly managed by actors, the National by Wallack, the Olympic by Mitchell, and Burton's, one of the best, by the British-born William Burton. The only serious rival of Burton's was Wallack's (formerly Brougham's Lyceum), opened in 1852 by another London actor, James Wallack, who left a son, Lester, and a nephew, James, to carry on his work. This they did with great success, James being at his best in tragedy and strong drama, Lester in comedy and romance. It was with this theatre that Dion Boucicault was mainly associated. Boucicault's American plays included the first, and for a long time the only attempt to treat the
Ill. 198 American Negro seriously on the stage, in *The Octoroon; or, Life in Lousiana*. In this the famous Joseph Jefferson, third of the name and a second-generation American, played Salem Scudder. Jefferson, whose charming, humorous personality, typical of all that was best in the American of his time, comes over admirably in his autobiography, was also excellent as Caleb Plummer in *The Cricket on the Hearth*,
Ill. 200 and as Bob Acres in *The Rivals*. But it is for his Rip Van Winkle that he is chiefly remembered. After appearing in an unsatisfactory

196

197 The American actor Edwin
Forrest (1806–72) in his most
famous role, Spartacus in *The
Gladiator* by Robert M. Bird

198 (*below*) The Slave Market
Scene in *The Octoroon; or, Life in
Louisiana*, in which the wealthy
young Southern girl tries to buy
Zoë, the octoroon. This play, by
Dion Boucicault (1822–90), was
first produced in the United States
in 1859, with Boucicault's wife
Agnes Robertson as Zoë and
Jefferson as Salem Scudder

version of Washington Irving's story, by several hands, he went to London in 1865 and there made a success in a dramatization by Boucicault which he so altered and adapted over the years that he made it virtually his own.

One of the parts which Jefferson created was Asa Trenchard in *Our American Cousin*. It was in this play that E. A. Sothern played Lord Dundreary and gave the English language a new name for drooping side-whiskers. Written by an Englishman, Tom Taylor, it was first produced in the United States by Laura Keene, a fine actress and theatre manager who in 1856 opened her own theatre in New York. This was a beautiful house with a white and gold interior, upholstered in gold damask. She prospered for a while, but was ruined by the outbreak of the War between the States, and went on tour. Her company was playing in *Our American Cousin* at Ford's Theatre in Washington, D.C. on 15 April 1865, when Lincoln was assassinated in his box by the younger brother of Edwin Booth, who was also an actor. There was a strong strain of insanity in the Booth family which in Edwin manifested itself in melancholia, and he never fully recovered from the shock of his brother's action. But as a tragic actor he had no equal. Both he and Jefferson, who was supreme in comedy, were the forerunners of a generation of American actors which included such figures as Mantell, Gillette, Mansfield, Mrs Fiske, Julia Marlowe and Maude Adams. One actress whose career spanned the greater part of the century and almost epitomized in itself the history of the early American stage was Mrs John Drew, for many years manager of the Arch Street Theatre, Philadelphia. As Louisa Lane, she appeared on the stage as a small child, playing in England with Macready, and in the United States with the first Joseph Jefferson. In her old age she matched the third Joseph Jefferson's Bob Acres with her own Mrs Malaprop, one of her best parts. Her son John and her grandchildren the Barrymores carried on the traditions of the family into the next century, John Barrymore in particular being renowned for his fine portrayal of Hamlet.

Ill. 199

As economic pressure forced the immigrants to the United States farther and farther west, actors accompanied or soon followed them, and it was not long before theatres were being built all over

198

199 (*above*) Mrs John Drew (1820–97) as Mrs Malaprop in Sheridan's *The Rivals*

200 Joseph Jefferson (1829–1905), third of the name, as Rip Van Winkle in the version prepared for him by Dion Boucicault, which he first played in London at the Adelphi in 1865, and in New York a year later

the continent, with companies moving from one to another. Among the pioneers were the Drakes, led by 'Old Sam' Drake; Caldwell, who built the first theatre in New Orleans; Ludlow and Sol Smith, who ran several theatres from their base in St Louis; the second Joseph Jefferson, who took his family to act in Chicago; and the lovely Julia Dean, grand-daughter of 'Old Sam' Drake, who made her début in Omaha. In Nauvoo, Illinois, where the Mormons first settled after they left New York, their leader Brigham Young played in *Pizarro*, and so encouraged the Mormon passion for play-acting that later in Salt Lake City they built a fine theatre, copied from Drury Lane, with a bust of Shakespeare over the door. In Colorado and far west on the Pacific coast the gold-miners demanded entertainment, paying for it in gold-dust. All the great names of the theatre flocked to California, where the first theatres were built in about 1850. The brightest star of them all was Charlotte Crabtree, known as Lotta, who toured the mining camps from the age of ten before going to New York to play in *Little Nell and the Marchioness*, *Ill. 201* and to make a fortune out of burlesques and extravaganzas. And down the Mississippi floated the showboats, pioneered by William Chapman, a London actor, and made famous by Edna Ferber's novel *Showboat* and the musical based on it. The staple fare of these floating theatres was melodrama and pantomime or such nautical dramas as *Black-Eyed Susan*. American playwrights were still few and far between, though Anna Cora Mowatt, who was also an actress, produced in *Fashion; or, Life in New York* the first American social comedy. But it was a long time before anyone rivalled the prolific Boucicault. Meanwhile, the craze for Negro minstrels swept

201 Charlotte Crabtree (1847–1924), known as Lotta, as the Marchioness, in a dramatization by John Brougham of Dickens' *Old Curiosity Shop* (1867)

202 (*far right*) John Drew (1853–1927), son of Mrs John Drew (*see Ill. 199*), and Ada Rehan (1860–1916) in *The Railroad of Love*, Daly's Theatre, New York, 1888

across the country and reached as far as England, rivalled in popularity only by spectacular song-and-dance shows like *The Black Crook* at Niblo's Garden, or by the variety show and its successor the vaudeville show, which reached its apotheosis at the Palace Theatre in New York.

Perhaps the nearest rival to Boucicault in the United States was Augustin Daly, whose ninety plays were mainly adaptations. He is however chiefly remembered for the theatres he opened in New York and London. The latter opened in 1893 with a production of *The Taming of the Shrew*, headed by Daly's leading players, John Drew and Ada Rehan. This theatre later became a fashionable home *Ill. 202* of musical comedy. Daly is also remembered for having encouraged Bronson Howard, the first American dramatist to make a living by

writing plays, by staging his initial effort, *Saratoga*. Howard's *Young Mrs Winthrop*, which marked a distinct advance in the development of native American drama, was later put on by Belasco, who like Daly was a prolific playwright and a manager who opened his own theatre in New York. His productions were spectacular, and in later life he was noted for his artistic use of stage lighting. His own plays had no literary value, but were excellent vehicles tailored to fit the players who made their names under his management. Among them were Mrs Leslie Carter in *Zaza*, Blanche Bates in *Madame Butterfly*, and David Warfield in Klein's *The Auctioneer*. The American theatre now had everything it needed except a great playwright. Clyde Fitch, though excellent in many ways, hardly qualified. His most popular plays were *Beau Brummell*, written for Richard Mansfield, and *Captain Jinks of the Horse Marines*, in which Ethel Barrymore scored her first success.

Curiously enough, it was an American manager, Hezekiah Bateman, who was to further the career of one of England's greatest actors. Seeking a theatre in which to display the talents of his *Ill. 204* daughters Kate, Virginia (who married an English actor and became the mother of Fay Compton), and Isabel, who had all been on the stage since early childhood, Bateman took over the London Lyceum in 1871 and engaged as his leading man the thirty-three-year-old *Ills. 205, 207* Henry Irving. Irving's career up to that time had given no indication of his future greatness. He was not a naturally good actor. His voice was harsh and his gait ungainly. Throughout his career there were always critics ready and anxious to point out his faults. But with the determination of genius he overcame all his handicaps and in so doing gained great personal prestige, being the first English actor to be knighted. He scored his first success at the Lyceum as Matthias *Ill. 205* in *The Bells*, a melodrama which he persuaded Bateman to put on when the season had opened disappointingly. This study in terror made him famous overnight, and his reputation was further enhanced by the pathos of his Charles I and by his controversial Hamlet. In 1879 he took over the management of the Lyceum himself, and made it the first theatre in London. As his leading lady he engaged *Ill. 207* Ellen Terry, the second daughter of a large theatrical family, and a

203 Fred Terry (1863–1933), as Henry in one of his most popular productions, *Henry of Navarre*, by William Devereux, first seen in 1908. Fred had his stage training under the Bancrofts (*Ill. 210*) and Irving (*Ills. 205, 207*)

much-loved actress who was considered the embodiment of all that was charming and womanly. She had been on the stage since early childhood, making her first appearance in Charles Kean's company at the age of ten. In the same company was her elder sister Kate, accounted by some a finer actress than Ellen, who retired early on marriage, and whose eldest daughter, also Kate, was the mother of John Gielgud. Ellen's youngest brother, Fred, was a fine romantic actor, who with his beautiful wife, Julia Neilson, appeared in such popular successes as *The Scarlet Pimpernel* and *Henry of Navarre*.

Ill. 203

To act with Irving was an education in itself, and among the young men he engaged and trained were William Terriss, later well-loved in nautical melodrama at the Adelphi, who was murdered outside the stage door by a madman, and whose daughter Ellaline, a delightful heroine in musical comedy, married the light comedian

204 Kate Bateman and her sister Ellen, aged eight and seven, in *The Young Couple*, specially adapted for them from *Le Mariage Enfantin*, by Eugène Scribe, in which they appeared during their season at the St James's Theatre, London, in 1851. They also played Portia and Shylock, Macbeth and Lady Macbeth, and Richard III and Richmond

205 (*above*) Henry Irving (1838–1905) as Mathias
in *The Bells*, a melodrama by Leopold Lewis
based on Erckmann-Chatrian's *Le Juif polonais*,
first produced at the Lyceum, London, in 1851.
Here Irving as the Burgomaster sees in a
vision the Polish Jew he has murdered and robbed

207 Irving and Ellen Terry (1847–1928) as
Iachimo and Imogen in *Cymbeline* at the Lyceum
in 1896. Irving took a great risk in putting on
such a little-known play, but it was a success.
Ellen Terry charmed the audience as Imogen, and
even Bernard Shaw, Irving's severest critic,
said of his Iachimo that it was 'a true impersona-
tion, without a single lapse in the sustained
beauty of its execution'

206 John Martin-Harvey (1863–1944) as Sidney Carton in *The Only Way*, an adaptation by several hands of Dickens' novel, *A Tale of Two Cities*. First produced at the Lyceum in 1899, it was an immediate success

Seymour Hicks; Johnston Forbes-Robertson, one of the finest
Ill. 208 Hamlets of all time, an actor of great delicacy and charm, with a
superb voice, who was knighted during his farewell appearance at
Ill. 191 Drury Lane (he was also a painter – one of his pictures is illustrated);
and John Martin-Harvey, also a great romantic actor. He is best
Ill. 206 remembered for one part, Sydney Carton in *The Only Way* (a
dramatization of *A Tale of Two Cities*), as is Wilson Barrett for his
Marcus Superbus in *The Sign of the Cross*, and Lewis Waller for his
Monsieur Beaucaire and d'Artagnan. These were the popular idols
of the day, particularly in the provinces, where the old stock companies had been dispersed, leaving the larger towns dependent on
visiting companies. The leading actors of the day toured extensively,
especially in the summer, as did the actor-managers Frank Benson
and Ben Greet with their Shakespeare companies. The first eventually established the Shakespeare Festival at Stratford-upon-Avon

208 Johnston Forbes-Robertson (1853–1937) as Hamlet in a production at the
Lyceum Theatre in September 1897. This shows the entry of Fortinbras in the
final scene

which was later to play so important a part in English theatrical life. The second took himself and his actors to the Old Vic, in the Waterloo Road, for many years Shakespeare's London home, and now the temporary home of the National Theatre Company.

The tradition of the actor-manager established in his own theatre, inaugurated by Irving, was carried on in London by George Alexander at the St James's Theatre, which he took over in 1891; by Beerbohm Tree at Her Majesty's, which he built in 1897 with the profits from his tenure of the Haymarket; and by Charles Wyndham, in the theatre which he built in 1899 and named after himself. In all these fine playhouses there was equally fine acting, but the plays were mostly fustian. Even Tom Taylor, whose *Ticket-of-Leave Man* *Ill. 209* was the best of many dramas of contemporary low life, cannot be accounted more than a good craftsman in the old style. It was a style which Tom Robertson, brother of the actress Madge Kendal,

209 A scene from *The Ticket-of-Leave Man* by Tom Taylor (1817–80), which had in it the first stage detective, Hawkshaw (*centre*), and also the first stage setting of a London restaurant

210 Squire Bancroft
(1841–1926) with his wife
Marie Wilton (1839–1921)
as Sidney Daryl and Maud
Hetherington in *Society*, the
first play of Tom Robertson,
which they produced under
their own management at
the Prince of Wales's Theatre
in 1865

was to destroy with his early efforts at realism in his so-called 'cup-
and-saucer' dramas. These were given at the Prince of Wales's
Ill. 210 Theatre by Marie Wilton and her husband, Squire Bancroft. They
demanded a complete revolution both in acting and in staging. The
heavy delivery and broad gestures of earlier days were superseded
by a quieter and more natural style of acting. The colourful but often
irrelevant décors inherited from melodrama were replaced by somewhat more realistic furniture and settings. Some of the effects of the
change-over can be seen in *Trelawny of the 'Wells'*, a light comedy by
A. W. Pinero, a playwright who startled Victorian playgoers as much
with *The Second Mrs Tanqueray* and *The Notorious Mrs Ebbsmith*
(which made the reputation of that fine but uneven actress, Mrs
Patrick Campbell, later the first Eliza Doolittle) as his contemporary
H. A. Jones did with *Saints and Sinners* and *Michael and his Lost Angel*.
Jones, who considered himself a leader in the Theatre of Ideas, was
also a good craftsman – the third act of his *Mrs Dane's Defence* is a
classic example of dramatic tension – but his plays are now for-

gotten. Of Pinero's works only his early farces are still acted and admired. Both men thought themselves realists and social critics, but both suffered from a tendency to run away from the issues they had raised, and their characters behaved more in accordance with the conventions of the theatre than with those of real life. They had none of the wit of the unclassifiable Oscar Wilde, whose brilliant and artificial comedies, of which the best is *The Importance of Being Earnest*, are still current on the stage, or of W. S. Gilbert, whose *Ill. 211* plays, popular in their own day, have been overshadowed by the success of his libretti for light opera (derived from the forgotten extravaganzas and burlesques of Planché) which are indissolubly linked with the music of Arthur Sullivan.

Jones and Pinero and countless other dramatists were influenced in their work by the French dramatist Victorien Sardou, who succeeded Scribe as the purveyor of high-class melodrama, described derisively by Bernard Shaw as 'Sardoodledum'. He wrote many of his plays for the French actress Sarah Bernhardt, the 'golden-voiced', who through her high-spirited unconventionality became a legend in her lifetime. But even those who smiled at her absurdities admitted the excellence of her acting, and she had a long and brilliant career which took her all over the world. Although at her best in emotional, melodramatic parts like Tosca and Fedora, she was willing to tackle

211 George Alexander as John Worthing and Allan Aynesworth as Algernon Moncrieff in the first production of Oscar Wilde's *The Importance of Being Earnest* at the St James's Theatre, London, on 14 February 1895

anything – Madame Sans-Gêne, Phèdre, Marguerite Gautier,
Ill. 212 L'Aiglon, even Hamlet and Pelléas. Her only rival on the Continent
was the Italian actress Eleonora Duse, for whom the plays of
d'Annunzio were written. At her best in tragedy, she was in many
ways the opposite of the flamboyant Sarah Bernhardt, quiet,

212 Sarah Bernhardt (1845–1923) and Mrs Patrick Campbell (*née* Beatrice Stella
Tanner, 1865–1940) as Pelléas and Mélisande in the 1904 production of the play
of that name by Maurice Maeterlinck

213 Eleonora Duse (1858–1924) as Magda in an Italian version of *Die Heimat* (1893) by Hermann Sudermann, at Drury Lane, London, in 1895

withdrawn, an actress of great strength and subtlety. An enigmatic person, who in seeming to shun publicity attracted it, she too travelled extensively. In 1895 she appeared in London as Magda in Sudermann's *Heimat*, playing in Italian at the same time as Bernhardt was playing the part in French. This gave playgoers the unusual opportunity of comparing the two interpretations on the spot, an unusual event celebrated by Bernard Shaw in a masterly article written as dramatic critic of *The Saturday Review*. He preferred Duse in the part.

Ill. 213

Die Heimat seemed new and daring when first produced, and a year later it was translated into English (as *Magda*) by Louis N. Parker. Shorn of the glamour of a foreign tongue and bereft of its equally glamorous leading ladies, it proved rather shoddy stuff, typical of much that passed for strong drama in the theatre of its day. But perhaps the actor-managers were less to blame than one might think in remaining faithful to the melodrama and romance their audiences demanded, since they had to face strong competition from the mushrooming music-hall. This form of entertainment, which

215 George Robey (1869–1954), known as 'The Prime Minister of Mirth', as Dame Hubbard in the pantomime *Goody-Two-Shoes*

214 (*left*) The famous music-hall star Marie Lloyd (1870–1922) in a characteristic costume and pose. Among her best-known songs were 'My Old Man said Follow the Van' and 'I'm One of the Ruins that Cromwell Knocked About a Bit'. She first appeared at the Royal Eagle Music Hall in 1885, and worked until a few days before her death

began modestly enough in the 1850s, soon created its own stars, who travelled incessantly from one town to another, and achieved enviable reputations. Some of them are still remembered – Vesta Tilley, Little Tich, Marie Lloyd, Grock, Harry Lauder, George Robey. They *Ills. 214, 215* were individualists, and had little in common with straight actors, but their work touched the theatre at one point, when music-hall comedians of the calibre of Dan Leno and Herbert Campbell appeared annually in the Christmas pantomime, and music-hall routines were incorporated into the story. It was this that finally led to the lengthening of the fairy-tale opening and the ousting of the last remnants of the Harlequinade once made glorious by the genius of Grimaldi, whose Clown owed nothing to Italian models, *Ill. 188* and was, like the pantomime itself, a purely English creation.

CHAPTER ELEVEN

Ibsen, Chekhov and the Theatre of Ideas

Although it is not necessary for the theatre as a medium of entertainment to concern itself seriously with social problems, or to look for plays of permanent literary value, there are times when, perhaps in memory of its religious origins, the tide turns against triviality and too great a divorce between reality and illusion. Audiences then demand – or perhaps it would be truer to say, are willing to accept – plays of social protest and criticism, even of propaganda. This may result in poor playwriting and in the production of a number of plays which, being nothing but propaganda, disappear without trace once their usefulness is over. But given the perfect balance between good theatre and a social problem of universal application, it may result in substantial additions to the world's stock of imperishable dramatic literature.

Such a period began in the European theatre of the late nineteenth century with the plays of Ibsen, reinforced by those of Chekhov. Both playwrights came from countries that had not previously made much impact on the European theatre. Denmark, whose history until 1814 was bound up with that of Norway, had produced a good writer of tragedy in the German style in Adam Oehlenschlaeger, and an excellent writer of comedy, mainly influenced by Molière and the *commedia dell'arte*, in Ludvig Holberg. But though both dramatists were known and acted throughout Europe, they had no following, and remained *sui generis*. It was not until Ibsen established a European reputation with *Brand*, one of his early verse-plays, of which the best known is *Peer Gynt*, that other countries thought of looking towards Scandinavia for inspiration. It came in full measure, first with the four searing pictures of small-town life, *The Pillars of Society*, *A Doll's House*, *Ghosts* and *An Enemy of the People*, and then with the symbolism of *The Wild Duck* and *The Master Builder* and the studies of individual exploration of experience in *Rosmersholm*, *Hedda*

Gabler, *Little Eyolf* and *John Gabriel Borkman*. Ibsen's last play, *Ill. 217*
When We Dead Awaken, is a powerful work, written at the age of
seventy. It is comparable in its wisdom and maturity to *The Tempest*,
the last play of Shakespeare, whom Ibsen approaches closely in the
profoundly poetic thought and form underlying even his most
realistic works.

Ibsen, who learned his stagecraft as assistant manager of the Bergen
and Oslo theatres, and through careful study of the German and
Italian theatres which he visited on his travels, had an immense
influence not only on the drama of his day but also on the art of
acting and scenic presentation. It was under his influence, combined
with that of the Meiningers, that Antoine, who did more than anyone to deliver Europe from the domination of the 'well-made' play,
founded the Théâtre Libre in Paris. Here he produced the first
French translation of *Ghosts*, playing Oswald himself. Later his
Théâtre Antoine became a rallying-point for young dramatists.
There, and at the Odéon, he produced such realistic masterpieces as
Becque's *La Parisienne* and Brieux's *Les Avariés*; as *Damaged Goods* *Ill. 216*
the latter created a sensation in England and the United States.
Antoine's influence, which continued into the next generation with
Jacques Copeau, led to the establishment in Germany of the Freie
Bühne under Otto Brahm, who encouraged the German dramatist
Gerhart Hauptmann, and of Grein's Independent Theatre in London,
where the battle for Ibsen was not won without a determined
struggle. The influential theatre critic Clement Scott denounced
Ghosts (in a translation by the equally eminent critic William Archer)
as a 'deplorably dull play. . . handled by a bungler', and 'an open
drain . . . a loathsome sore unbandaged', 'a dirty act done publicly . . .
a lazarhouse with all its doors and windows open'. But with the
co-operation of such actresses as Janet Achurch, the first Nora in *A* *Ill. 217*
Doll's House, and Elizabeth Robins, the first Hedda Gabler, Hilda
(in *The Master Builder*) and Rebecca West (in *Rosmersholm*), Ibsen
was eventually established on the English stage. In the United
States he met with less opposition, partly owing to the leavening
effect of a number of Scandinavian immigrants in the audience, and
partly to the absence of an effective censorship. The first production

to arouse widespread interest was *A Doll's House*, with Beatrice Cameron as Nora. It also aroused the hostility of the critic William Winter, who, like Scott, defended the old drama against this unwholesome importation from Europe. But again Ibsen triumphed, with the help of Mrs Fiske, Blanche Bates and Alla Nazimova. It is interesting in this connection to note how many of Ibsen's finest parts are written for women.

The only other Scandinavian dramatists to compare with Ibsen were his fellow-countryman and contemporary Bjørnson, and the younger Swedish dramatist, Strindberg. Bjørnson, like Ibsen, worked in the Bergen and Oslo theatres, and his plays often deal with the same moral diseases of contemporary society. But he differs from Ibsen in his optimism and his firmly expressed belief in a redemptive force. Some of his plays, notably *Beyond Human Power*, have been seen in England, but most of them, being more immediate and less universal in their application than Ibsen's, are less accessible to an English audience, and his main influence has been on the Continent, particularly in Germany.

Strindberg, who brought vitality into Swedish drama, provoked at first almost as much hostility as Ibsen. His plays were slower to establish themselves in translation, but *The Father, Miss Julie* and *The Dance of Death* have now been recognized as masterpieces which explore abnormal states of mind and denounce by implication not so much the accidental corruption of society as certain basic evils in the human heart. On the technical side Strindberg made many innovations in the theatre. Through the work done at the Intima Teatern which he founded in Stockholm with his third wife, the actress Harriet Bosse, for the production of his own plays, he had a widespread influence on the theatre of his day, and anticipated much of the technical virtuosity later fashionable in Europe and the United States.

The Independent Theatre, which first brought *Ghosts* to London, also put on the first play of the Irish playwright George Bernard Shaw. Shaw, who was an ardent disciple of Ibsen, was the implacable enemy of the type of theatre so much enjoyed by Clement Scott, and abominated the productions of Irving at the Lyceum. His own

216 (*above*) A reading to an invited audience at the Théâtre Antoine of *Les Avariés* by its author, Eugène Brieux, in 1901 – a protest against censorship

217 The visit of the Rat-Wife, a scene from *Little Eyolf*, by Henrik Ibsen, in the first English production at the Avenue Theatre, London, in 1896. Mrs Patrick Campbell played the Rat-Wife, Janet Achurch was Rita and Elizabeth Robins Asta

plays were at first considered almost as subversive as Ibsen's, since they were concerned with social problems, such as slum landlordism and prostitution, which were judged unfit for public discussion. He aimed his arguments at the audience's intelligence rather than at its emotions, and though some of his plays failed to maintain their place in the repertory once the abuses that occasioned them were corrected, most have been successful in revival. Even his most blatant propaganda is presented with wit and elegance, and his plays in general are based on a sound knowledge of theatre technique. Shaw's long career stretched from *Widowers' Houses* in 1892 to *Buoyant Billions* in 1949. During this time he dominated the stage not

218 Richard Mansfield (1857–1907) as Dick Dudgeon in *The Devil's Disciple* by George Bernard Shaw (1856–1950), which had its world première in a performance at the Guild Theatre, New York, in 1897

219 (*right*) Sybil Thorndike as Saint Joan in the first London production (1924) of Shaw's play of that name, at the New Theatre. Here Joan waits with Dunois and his page for a west wind to carry their army across the Loire

only in England, but on the Continent, where many of his plays had their first productions in translation. *Caesar and Cleopatra* was first seen in Berlin, *Pygmalion* in Vienna, *The Apple Cart* in Warsaw, *Buoyant Billions* in Zurich. One of the best known of his early plays, *The Devil's Disciple*, was given its first production in New York, with Richard Mansfield in the part of Dick Dudgeon. Among other *Ill. 218* plays seen first in the United States were *Heartbreak House, Back to Methuselah*, and *Saint Joan*, which is usually considered Shaw's finest work. The part of St Joan was played in London by Sybil *Ill. 219* Thorndike, who with her husband Lewis Casson has had a long and distinguished career on the English stage.

It was Harley Granville-Barker who first made Shaw known to the general public in England by producing eleven of his plays at the Court Theatre during the season of 1906-7. Barker had already made a name for himself as a producer of Shakespeare in the new simplified style introduced by William Poel in reaction against the elaborate staging of Irving and Tree, in which the text was often sacrificed to the scenery. Most of Poel's productions were given in halls in which he tried to reproduce the conditions of the Elizabethan stage as he understood them, but occasionally he made use of a theatre, setting up an Elizabethan stage within the proscenium arch. Poel's work was of capital importance in the development of

Ill. 220

Shakespearian production and its repercussions are still being felt today. He was a good actor, and played Father Keegan in Shaw's *John Bull's Other Island*. But he himself said that he preferred stage management to acting, and it is as a producer that he is remembered. As well as Shakespeare, he produced a modernized version of the old Morality play *Everyman*, with which he toured extensively in England and the United States.

The first of Shaw's plays to be shown in public was *Arms and the Man* in 1894, which was included in her season at the Avenue Theatre by Florence Farr, who played Louka. The financial backing was provided by Miss Horniman, a remarkable woman, who founded

220 A production of *Hamlet* by the pioneer of simplified staging, William Poel (1852-1934), at the Carpenters' Hall, London, in February 1900. Poel played Hamlet

221 A scene from the Moscow Art Theatre's 1902 production of *The Lower Depths* by Maxim Gorki, directed by Stanislavsky who can be seen far back stage right

222 (*right*) Shaw's *Androcles and the Lion*, from the first production at the St James's ▶ Theatre, London, by Harley Granville-Barker in 1913

the Abbey Theatre in Dublin, a venture which achieved a high standard of acting whose influence was widespread, and was ultimately responsible for the plays of J. M. Synge and Sean O'Casey. Miss Horniman also introduced the idea of the modern repertory theatre into England from the Continent, where she had seen and admired it in action. From 1908 to 1917 she maintained at the Gaiety Theatre in Manchester a company which provided the inspiration for the Liverpool and Birmingham Repertory theatres. The latter was the creation of Barry Jackson, who also founded the Malvern Festival for the production of Shaw's plays, and introduced Shakespeare in modern dress to London audiences with *Hamlet* in 1925 and *Macbeth* in 1928, both transferred from Birmingham.

One of Shaw's plays, *Heartbreak House*, is labelled 'a fantasia in the Russian manner'. This is a tribute to Chekhov, whose *Cherry Orchard* Shaw had persuaded the Stage Society to put on in London in 1912. It was the English playgoer's first introduction to the work of Russia's greatest dramatist of pre-Revolutionary days. Like all dramatists with something new to offer, Chekhov needed new-style actors to interpret him. He found them, after some initial failures elsewhere, in the company founded by Stanislavsky and Nemirovich- *Ills. 221, 223* Danchenko at the Moscow Art Theatre.

Before the advent of Stanislavsky, whose formulated 'method' of training actors has become the theatrical bible of modern America, the Russian theatre had developed unnoticed outside its own borders. It had excellent actors – Shchepkin, Mochalov, Karatygin – many of them serfs trained in the private playhouses maintained by wealthy noblemen. It also had good plays, the result of the founding of a specifically Russian literature by the poet Pushkin. Among them were Lermontov's tragedy *Maskerad*, the comedies of Griboyedov, Gogol and Ostrovsky, and Turgeniev's *A Month in the Country*. But all these, together with the plays of Tolstoi and of Gorki, the 'stormy *Ill. 221* petrel' of the Revolution whose best work had to wait for production

223 The company of the Moscow Art Theatre, founded in 1898 by Nemirovich-Danchenko and Stanislavsky (*see also Ill. 221*), listening to a reading by Chekhov of his play *The Seagull*, in which they appeared in 1899. Stanislavsky, who played Trigorin, is sitting on Chekhov's right, Nemirovich-Danchenko is standing far left

until after 1917, had made no impact on Europe. It was not until Stanislavsky had trained actors able to convey the subtlety of Chekhov's dialogue, which had seemed incomprehensible when presented in the old style of acting, that first Russia and then the world acknowledged his greatness. In the same way, when Chekhov was first acted in English he was, though much admired, completely misunderstood. Subsequent revivals and new translations have revealed him more fully, and he has had a great influence on English writers as well as on producers and actors. His influence has been equally marked throughout Europe and the United States.

Shortly after the founding of Antoine's Théâtre Libre, Adrià Gual founded in Barcelona the Teatro Intim, in the hope of introducing Ibsen to Spain, but with little success. Ibsen's influence shows itself most strongly in Echegaray's *El gran Galeoto* and *El hijo de*

Don Juan, based on *Ghosts*; but the work of Spain's best-known dramatist of this period, Jacinto Benavente, a versatile and original writer who was awarded the Nobel Prize for Literature in 1922, seems, at least in such plays as *Los intereses creados* (known in English as *The Bonds of Interest*), to derive more from Shakespeare and the *commedia dell'arte*. And the plays of the Quintero brothers, familiar through the translations of Granville-Barker, are more representative of the sentimental strain found in the Catalán theatre than of modern realism. This is true too of Martínez Sierra, whose *Cradle Song* and *Romantic Young Lady* have proved popular far beyond Spain, in fact more popular sometimes abroad than in his own country. It should however be remembered that Martínez Sierra, who for some years ran the Eslava Theatre, was the first to appreciate and produce the plays of García Lorca, a potentially important

225

224 The Italian actor Ernesto Rossi (1827–96) as Hamlet at Drury Lane in 1876, in an Italian version which he first performed in Italy in *c.* 1857

225 (*right*) Probably the most popular of Pirandello's plays: *Six Characters in Search of an Author*, first seen in Italy in 1921, and in England in 1922; here seen in a production at the Arts Theatre Club in 1928 ▶

playwright who was killed in the Spanish Civil War, and who is best remembered for his three tragedies, *Blood Wedding*, *The House of Bernarda Alba* and *Yerma*.

Ill. 224   Italy, under the joint influence of Ibsen and Shakespeare, who had been introduced to Italian audiences by the tragic actor Ernesto Rossi, and in reaction against the plays of Gabriele d'Annunzio, now produced the dramatist Pirandello, who achieved a dominant position in the theatre of the twentieth century. Neither the poverty of his early years nor the later tragedy of his wife's insanity had the power to quench his love for the theatre. In 1925 he established a company in Rome at the Teatro Odescalchi with Ruggero Ruggeri and Marta Abba as its leading players, and produced there his own plays, which deal with the illusion of life and the hopelessness of man's attempts to recognize reality. There can be no truth, says Pirandello, since truth varies with the individual and the circumstances; there can be no communication, since words interpret what seems to be, and not what is; there can be no sanity, for sanity demands stability, which is not to be found in the human condition. The influence of Pirandello's philosophy on the disillusioned generation of the 1920s and 1930s was profound, and has not yet expended all its force. Though *Enrico IV* is probably his finest play, the best known in translation are *Six Characters in Search of an Author, As You Desire Me,* *Right You Are If You Think You Are,* and *Tonight We Improvise.* *Ill. 225*

The new drama naturally demanded a new approach to scenic design as well as to acting, and a pioneer of the new movement, which was to be particularly successful in the United States, was the Swiss artist Adolphe Appia. Shocked by the disparity between the two-dimensional scenery and the three-dimensional actor, he endeavoured to design settings eloquent in their simplicity which would provide the actor not with a background but with an environment. His admirable sets were enhanced by dramatic lighting effects made possible by the introduction of electricity and the many subsequent discoveries of ways in which to employ and control it, including the use of the cyclorama. *Ill. 227*

Another and even more powerful advocate of scenic simplicity, and one whose writings and teaching were to have an influence on

226 (*left*) A set for *Macbeth* ('So foul and fair a day I have not seen') from a series designed by Edward Gordon Craig (1872–1966) for a production at the Knickerbocker Theater, New York, in 1928

228 Gordon Craig's set for Act II (The Banqueting Hall) of Ibsen's *Kongsemnerne* (*The Crown Pretenders*)

227 (*below left*) A set for Act II of Ibsen's *Little Eyolf* (1924) by the Swiss designer Adolphe Appia (1862–1928). Appia and Craig between them revolutionized the art of scenic design in Europe and America, partly under the influence of the ◀ theatre of the Far East

the theatre everywhere out of all proportion to the amount of stage work he actually did, was Ellen Terry's son, Edward Gordon Craig. *Ills. 226, 228* He began his career as an actor in Irving's company, but finding himself unable to work freely in the English commercial theatre of the early twentieth century, he settled on the Continent, spending most of his long life (he died in 1966 at the age of ninety-four) battling against what he considered the egotism and stupidity of the actor, the inadequacy of the producer, and the crudity of the usual scene-designer. His system, in essentials, resolved itself into a series of large screens which served as a background for the imaginative use of changing lights. These, with a few moveable rostrums and flights of steps, were used to build up a stage picture which made no concession whatever to the prevailing passion for realism as envisaged by Stanislavsky at the Moscow Art Theatre, for instance. Nothing could be less like the general furbishings of the early twentieth-century stage, conditioned as it was almost everywhere by theatres built a hundred years previously. The theatre, more than any other art, suffers from having to work in solid architecture which keeps it always out of step with advanced ideas. Craig complained that there was no one in the theatre 'who is a master in himself, that is to say, there is no one man capable of inventing and rehearsing a play; capable of designing and superintending the construction of both scenery and costume; of writing any necessary music; of inventing such machinery as is needed and the lighting that is to be used'. To realize his conception it would be necessary to start again from the beginning, redesigning the theatre building and re-educating the actor.

A form of theatrical presentation which influenced Craig and other designers, as well as playwrights like Yeats, was that of the Far East, which, dating back beyond the oldest manifestations of theatre in modern Europe, remained virtually unknown there until the end of the nineteenth century. It was not the performances themselves which had any influence, for few Europeans had the opportunity of seeing them, but accounts of them by travellers and the translations of some of the play-texts by scholars like Arthur Waley. Reformers who wished to clear the stage of its nineteenth-century clutter were attracted by the appearance of simplicity – mistakenly, since both Chinese and Japanese productions are exceedingly complex – and by the use of symbolism which, in the reaction against realism, seemed to offer the European stage-designer a way out of the dead end in which he found himself.

It is almost impossible for the European mind to adjust itself to the traditional and ritual elements in the Far Eastern theatre. But there is much in it that anyone must admire. Particularly interesting are the evocative symbolism of the stage setting and the extremely beautiful costumes, where every colour and every fold of the material conveys a message; and the incredible artistry of the actors, trained from childhood in a severe discipline which gives them complete control of every gesture of the hands, every turn of the head and every movement of the body.

229 A scene from a Japanese Nōh play, *The Lady Aoi*, seen at the Aldwych Theatre, London, during the World Theatre Season of 1967. A priest (*stage left*) wrestles symbolically with an evil spirit for the life of the Lady Aoi

230 (*below*) A *kyōgen*, or comic interlude, *The Tied Servants*. Two servants, though tied up as shown in the picture, manage to steal wine from a large cask. London 1967

231 An eighteenth-century print of a Japanese *kabuki* theatre, showing the

hanamichi, or 'flower way', along which the actors make their entrances and exits

The Japanese theatre takes two forms (apart from the puppet-theatre, which cannot be dealt with here). There is the classical and
Ill. 229 aristocratic Nōh play, with its roots deep in religious ritual, and the
Ills. 231, 232 popular *kabuki*, a composite form whose ingredients are indicated by its name (*ka* – singing, *bu* – dancing, *ki* – acting). The Nōh is essentially a drama of soliloquy and reminiscence, with no action or development through conflict as in Western drama. As in ancient Greece, the chief actor (there are only two) is masked, and the satyr-
Ill. 230 play of Greek tragedy is paralleled by the *kyōgen* or comic interlude, which with its miming and clowning is strangely reminiscent of the atellan farce and the *commedia dell'arte*. The subjects of the Nōh play are taken from myth and legend. The actor, who is both singer and dancer, chants his lines and glides to and fro in a stately manner. The stamping of his stockinged feet on the resonant pinewood floor of the stage combines with the piercing notes of the transverse flute and the beat of the three drums to provide a rhythmic accompaniment to the action. The costumes of the actors are sumptuous, heavily embroidered and brilliantly coloured. This is true also of the costumes of the *kabuki*, which takes its subjects from history or from daily life. The actors, who are more numerous than in the Nōh play, are not masked, and their movements are, in comparison, freer and more sweeping, though still highly stylized. As in the Nōh play, there is a chorus of singers, and in addition an orchestra of samisen-players. One feature of the *kabuki* which had a great impact on Western stagecraft was the revolving stage, first installed at Munich in 1896 by Karl Lautenschläger. A detail from both types of play which intrigued a theatre habituated to complete realism on stage was the use of stage-hands (in blue or black kimonos), by tradition considered invisible, who were always ready to assist with costume changes, arrange the folds of a heavy skirt, or hand over and remove stage properties as required.

In Japan today, where the Nōh and the *kabuki* still flourish – the latter in modernized form – there has been some counter-influence from the West, and Shakespeare's plays have been performed on an 'Elizabethan' stage, modelled on the Fortune, erected at Waseda University, Tokyo, under the direction of Dr Tsubouchi, who translated them. New European plays have also been given, and efforts have been made to encourage the writing of plays in Japanese dealing realistically with modern problems. The old-fashioned style of acting has been found unsuitable for such tentatives, and training in Stanislavsky's 'method' has now been undertaken. The problem is rendered more complex by the fact that in both the *Nōh* and the *kabuki* the play is subordinate to the actor, whereas the modern European theatre has sought to subordinate the actor to the play, which the performer has the duty of interpreting for the audience. Perhaps the solution will come through the adaptation and extension of the comic *kyōgen*, which certainly deals realistically with life, *Ill. 230* though not as yet with the life of today.

232 A modern *kabuki* play, *Kanjinchō*, at the Kabuki-za Theatre in Tokyo in 1960; a revival in modern style of one of the most representative classical Japanese plays, first performed in 1840. The actors are Koshiro VIII as Benkei and Danjūrō XI as Togashi

The Chinese theatre, which since the beginning of the nineteenth century has consisted chiefly of the Peking opera, is also primarily designed for the actor. Its plays are a flexible and harmonious combination of dialogue, song, dance and acrobatics on subjects taken from national history, legends and fiction. Costumes, particularly those of the warriors, are magnificent, but make no attempt at historical accuracy. Colours indicate rank. Yellow is for an emperor, red for officials, black for rough men. Temperament is shown by conventional lines drawn on the face, and by a coloured make-up. Blue indicates ferocity, red loyalty and courage. There is an orchestra

236

233 (*left*) A scene from a Chinese play illustrating the symbolism by which the waving of blue flags indicates the sea

234 The heroine in a Chinese play (played by a man). The tasselled whip which she is carrying indicates that she is supposed to be on horseback

on the stage, but no scenery, and simple properties have with the lapse of time acquired certain symbolic values. A table is a bridge, three chairs a bed; an oar stands for a ship, a whip for a horse. Black flags mean a high wind, blue flags the waves of the sea, yellow flags a chariot. A fan is a sign of frivolity, a woman's tiny shoe represents needlework. A folded red cloak on the floor is a corpse. As in Japan, all the parts in a Chinese play were originally played by men, who started their training at an early age. The only Chinese actor known by name outside his own country was the female impersonator Mei Lan-Fang, who toured the United States, Europe and Russia in some

Ill. 234
Ill. 233

Ill. 235

237

235 Mei Lan-Fang (1894–1961) in one of his female parts. He was the first Chinese actor to combine the dramatic techniques of the five female roles in Peking opera, and his virtuosity, while only in his early twenties, caused the part of the heroine to oust the elderly bearded male from its pre-eminent place for the first time

of his finest parts, astonishing audiences everywhere by the delicacy and virtuosity of his performances in the five female roles of the Peking opera. In recent years actresses have been introduced into the companies, and efforts have been made throughout the country to encourage the reform and survival of many types of local theatre which have each its own repertory and characteristic style of music and acting. The influence of Western drama was apparent in the early twentieth century, when the works of Ibsen and other European dramatists were performed in translation, but since 1949 new plays have been mainly concerned with revolutionary propaganda. Although it is difficult to discover what is happening at the moment in China, the traditional theatre appears to have survived, and in the early 1960s a Peking opera company made a successful tour of Europe and Canada.

One or two Chinese plays have passed in adaptation into the dramatic literature of Europe. The first was *The Chinese Orphan*, used by Voltaire for his *L'Orphelin de la Chine*. The German drama- *Ill. 160* tist Klabund translated *The Chalk Circle*, which has been seen also in English, and in the 1930s both England and the United States enjoyed performances of *Lady Precious Stream*, adapted by the Chinese dramatist S. I. Hsiung.

The theatre of India, which is as ancient as that of China and Japan, and equally traditional, is little known in Europe, though her dance forms and music are becoming increasingly popular. The only plays known in translation are the fourth-century *Little Clay Cart*, attributed to Sūdraka, and the fifth-century *Śakuntalā*, by Kālidāsa. A translation of the latter, by Sir William Jones, published in 1789, first drew the attention of European readers to Sanskrit dramatic literature, and evoked the admiration of Goethe. It was produced in London in 1899. In modern times the plays of the Indian poet Rabindranath Tagore have been published and read, but seldom acted.

CHAPTER TWELVE

The Modern Theatre

With the works of Ibsen, Chekhov, Shaw and Pirandello the dramatist became paramount in the theatre. In order to survive the actor had to adapt himself to the new conditions which this entailed. Realistic dialogue demanded a quiet conversational style in place of the earlier rhetoric and declamation. Gestures had to become more restrained. The set had to be carefully designed to be as accurate as possible, with furniture and properties suitable to the place and period of the play. The illusion of reality was greatly helped by the almost universal adoption of the enclosed box-set, which had already begun to supersede the romantic backcloth and wings used in melodrama. It was adopted even for plays written for the open stage and an unlocalized setting, like those of Shakespeare, which suffered from having to be crammed behind a proscenium arch.

Zola's definition of a play as 'a slice of life', and the uncompromising naturalism of his own *Thérèse Raquin* (1873), helped to establish the new stagecraft. It spread rapidly all over Europe, and reached its zenith with the Moscow Art Theatre's production of *Ill. 221* Gorki's *Lower Depths* in 1902. In the United States its influence was *Ill. 236* seen in O'Neill's *Anna Christie* and *Desire Under the Elms*, and it inspired the ingenious stage devices patented by Steele MacKaye. It is one of the paradoxes of the theatre that the more realistic the play becomes the more it demands in the way of accessories. Shakespeare can be acted with 'bare boards and a passion'. But the realistic playwright demands all the clutter of daily living and, in addition, the separation of the audience from the actors. This led to the darkening of the auditorium and to the convention by which the proscenium arch became a 'fourth wall' through which the spectators watched the development of a remote action without becoming involved in it. It also had the effect of narrowing the dramatist's range to subjects which lent themselves to intimate domestic interior scenes.

236 Eben (played by Charles Ellis) with Abbie, his young stepmother (Mary Morris) in a scene from *Desire Under the Elms*, by Eugene O'Neill (1888–1953), first produced at the Greenwich Village Theatre in 1924 by the Provincetown Players, in a multiple set designed by Robert Edmond Jones

Too much insistence on realism was bound to produce a reaction. This took the form of expressionism, an hallucinatory vision of life evident in Strindberg's later plays. It originated in Germany, where it resulted in the plays of Wedekind and Kaiser. Its repercussions in France produced the plays of Lenormand. O'Casey's *Silver Tassie* and *Within the Gates* show its influence in England, O'Neill's *Emperor Jones* and *The Hairy Ape* in the United States. But although the expressionist play, veering as it does between conscious and subconscious states of mind, posed problems for actor and producer alike, it was mainly a literary manifestation. A reaction which, like that of Craig and Appia, struck at the roots of the realistic theatre, was constructivism, offspring of the Russian Revolution. This sought to re-establish the primacy of the actor, and to subordinate the setting to his theatrical needs. It abolished the detailed scenery of the realistic play in favour of non-realistic platforms, steps and significant forms, which were meant to convey to the audience the mechanical and *Ill. 237* dynamic qualities of contemporary Russian life. Meyerhold, with his theory of 'bio-mechanics', went even further, clearing the stage right to the back wall so as to leave a bare space on which he could manœuvre his actors like puppets.

Ill. 238   Expressionism and constructivism, the one literary, the other theatrical, served their turn and were superseded by other forms of theatre. Both movements were symptomatic of the search for a non-realistic theatre which would bring back to the playhouse the sense of wonder and participation temporarily lost in the desire for realism. Once the excitement engendered by the new realistic drama had

subsided, it was found that even Ibsen and Chekhov, hailed as the masters of realism, were also poets and symbolists. With Chekhov in particular, this necessitated a new approach to his plays to allow for the humour and fantasy inherent in his dialogue in addition to their detailed realism.

The so-called 'new drama' represents only a fraction of the plays written and performed during the period of its ascendancy. In reaction against it were the romantic dramas of Rostand, the fantasies of Maeterlinck, and the whimsical plays of James Barrie, which ran side by side with the brittle comedies of Noël Coward and the well-made and immensely popular comedies of Somerset Maugham. Austria had her own brand of cynicism with Arthur Schnitzler, but her best dramatist at this period was Hugo von Hofmannsthal, a prolific author who is sometimes in danger of being remembered only as the librettist of Richard Strauss. He was however equally active in his collaboration with Max Reinhardt, for whose Salzburg Festival he adapted the old Morality play, *Everyman*, and based *Das Salzburger grosse Welttheater* on Calderón's *El gran teatro del mundo*.

◀ 237 (*left*) A revolutionary stage in Soviet Russia in the 1920s: a production of Ostrovsky's *The Forest* (first produced in 1851), directed and designed by V. E. Meyerhold (1874–1943)

238 A constructivist set from the United States: the setting for O'Neill's *Dynamo* (1929), designed by Lee Simonson (1888–1967)

Mention of Reinhardt entails consideration of one of the outstanding phenomena of the twentieth-century theatre, the rise of the
producer, known in the United States as the director, and on the
Continent as the *régisseur*, though the French word implies much
more than its English equivalent. The evolution of ensemble acting
needed in the plays of Ibsen and Chekhov, and even in earlier times
the integrated style aimed at by the Meiningers, called for direction
by someone not actively engaged in the production. In this sense the
Duke of Saxe-Meiningen, who was never an actor, was probably the
first modern stage director. His successors have usually begun as
actors, and only later devoted themselves entirely to directing.

The first modern director to make an international reputation was
Max Reinhardt, for Stanislavsky, though earlier in time, was not
well known until later in his career. It was Reinhardt's reputation
which led indirectly to the fashion of attributing productions to the
director rather than to the leading actor or the author. Terminology
in these matters is a useful guide to the relative importance of the
elements involved in the presentation of a play. A study of the
differences between the Hamlets of Shakespeare, Garrick and
Reinhardt would reveal much about the workings of the theatre at
any given moment. One must now reckon also with the stage-
designer and costumier, who sometimes carries off the honours and
draws audiences to see his creations rather than the play they were
created for. There are even signs that lighting, especially in the United
States, will soon rank high in the scale, and we may yet be called
upon to admire an interpretation of *Hamlet* by the lighting expert.

Craig, in his desire for artistic unity in the presentation of a play,
had envisaged a theatre completely controlled by one man. Reinhardt
came closer than anyone to realizing this ideal. He dominated the
theatre of Central Europe for over twenty-five years, refusing to be
confined within the proscenium arch, and setting his plays in a ball-
room, a circus, a cathedral square, or an exhibition hall – anywhere,
in fact, where he could find space for his grandiose projects. The
Ill. 239 most memorable of them was *The Miracle*, a vast spectacle whose
crowds he manipulated with consummate ease. Yet he could produce
with equal artistry delicate intimate plays whose natural home was

244

the jewel-like Residenztheater in Munich. He was all-embracing in his use of scenery too, choosing permanent, semi-permanent or simultaneous settings as best suited his conception of the play, and adding to them runways, rostrums, steps and revolving stages. His extensive travels brought him into prominence everywhere. He finally settled in the United States in 1933, and remained there until his death ten years later. His gift for controlling an actor and bringing out the best in him was nowhere more apparent than in his handling of Moissi, who did such magnificent work as his leading man for many years, but failed to reach a comparable standard when Reinhardt's guiding hand was withdrawn.

Although the director is a comparative newcomer in the history of the theatre, many men have already made reputations in this field, and each has brought to his work some quality which marks a production as peculiarly his own. Among the outstanding British producers are Tyrone Guthrie, at his best in the handling of crowd scenes; Peter Brook, an infant prodigy who by-passed the usual formative stage of acting and directed his first production at eighteen; and Peter Ustinov, who in the old tradition directs and appears in his own plays. In France Jean-Louis Barrault, with his wife Madeleine Renaud, did good work with his own company, particularly in the *Ill. 240* production of Claudel's plays, and now heads France's second theatre, formerly the Odéon. The work of Antoine was carried on by Pitoëff and his wife Ludmilla at the Mathurins, and between the two world wars there was a famous quartet of directors in Paris – Charles Dullin at the Atelier, Jacques Copeau at the Vieux-Columbier, Gaston Baty at the old Montparnasse to which he gave his own name, and Louis Jouvet at the Athénée. Besides being an inspired interpreter of Molière's plays, Jouvet was responsible for bringing before the *Ill. 241* public the plays of Giraudoux, a witty and subtle dramatist whose *Ill. 244* works include *Ondine*, in which he handled the legend of the water-nymph in love with a mortal with all the poetry of which he was capable, and all the stage effects which he knew Jouvet could provide for him.

A Frenchman who has won international renown as a director is Copeau's nephew, Michel Saint-Denis, founder of the Compagnie

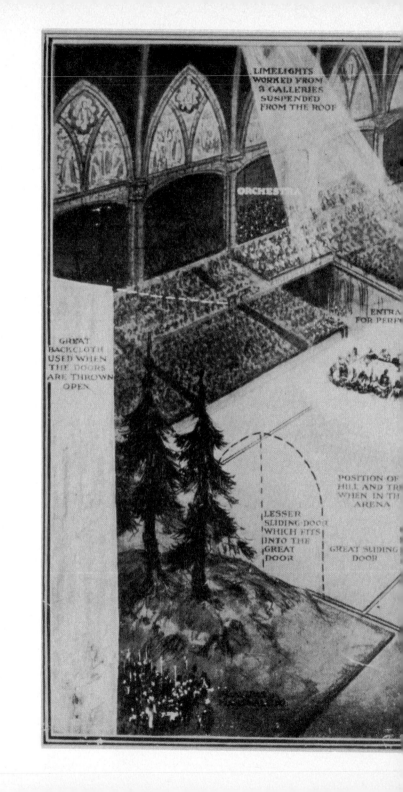

LIMELIGHTS
WORKED FROM
3 GALLERIES
SUSPENDED
FROM THE ROOF

ORCHESTRA

ENTRA
FOR PERFO

GREAT
BACKCLOTH
USED WHEN
THE DOORS
ARE THROWN
OPEN

POSITION OF
HILL AND TRE
WHEN IN TH
ARENA

LESSER
SLIDING DOOR
WHICH FITS
INTO THE
GREAT
DOOR

GREAT SLIDING
DOOR

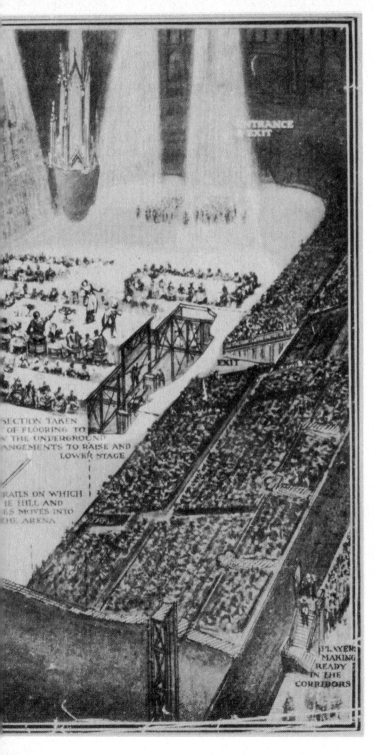

Within the illustration the following labels appear:

ENTRANCE & EXIT

EXIT

SECTION TAKEN
OF FLOORING TO
THE UNDERGROUND
ARRANGEMENTS TO RAISE AND
LOWER STAGE

RAILS ON WHICH
THE HILL AND
MOVES INTO
THE ARENA

PLAYERS
MAKING
READY
IN THE
CORRIDORS

239 A view from the flies of the Great Hall at Olympia, London, as it appeared during the production of *The Miracle* by Max Reinhardt (1873–1943) in 1911. This wordless spectacle-play by Karl Volmöller, with music by Engelbert Humperdinck, was based on an old legend about a nun who escapes from her convent and returns after many years to find that the Madonna has taken her place

240 (*above left*) Madeleine Renaud
and her husband Jean-Louis Barrault
in *Le Chien du Jardinier*, by
Georges Neveux, London 1956

242 (*above right*) The opening scene
of *King Lear* at Stratford-upon-
Avon, 1937, designed and
produced by Theodore
Komisarjevsky (1882–1954)

241 Louis Jouvet (1887–1951), one
of the outstanding figures of the
French theatre between the two
world wars, as Molière's Tartuffe

des Quinze and an excellent actor. Through his drama centres in London and Strasbourg he has been responsible for the training of many young actors, and he is active both in London and in New York. His peripatetic career, with its consequent cross-fertilization of the theatre on both sides of the Atlantic, was paralleled by that of Komisarjevsky, a Russian-born stage-designer and director who was one of the first to produce Chekhov's plays in London. He aroused fierce controversy with his productions of Shakespeare at Stratford-upon-Avon, particularly his *Macbeth*, with its aluminium scenery, and his *King Lear*, which finally established his reputation. *Ill. 242*

The first outstanding directors of Soviet Russia were Meyerhold; Vakhtangov, whose short but stimulating career in his own theatre in Moscow had widespread influence; Taïrov, who with his actress-wife Alice Koonen introduced to the Soviet stage the works of many contemporary foreign dramatists; and Okhlopkov, who was profoundly influenced by the theatrical concepts of the Far East. In Germany Jessner, who was one of the first to abolish scenery in favour of linked flights of steps providing different acting levels, and Piscator, a disciple of Reinhardt and the precursor of 'epic' theatre, were responsible for productions whose influence spread far beyond their own country. Piscator, like Reinhardt and Komisarjevsky, settled in the United States, which, being now fully-fledged, was able to produce her own directors. Among the first was Guthrie McClintic, who did some of his best work for plays which starred his wife, Katharine Cornell. This fine actress will always be associated with Elizabeth in *The Barretts of Wimpole Street*, as in earlier days Laurette Taylor was with Peg in her husband's play *Peg o' my Heart*.

243 R. E. Jones' setting for O'Neill's *Mourning Becomes Electra*, based on the *Oresteia* of Aeschylus, but transferred to a New England setting during the American Civil War. First produced at the Guild Theatre, New York, in 1931

Another well-known director today is Elia Kazan, who was responsible for the staging of plays by two of the United States' best modern playwrights, Arthur Miller and Tennessee Williams, among them the former's *After the Fall* and the latter's *Camino Real*. But it was in the field of scenic design that the American theatre first made its mark, with a succession of artists which included Lee Simonson, Norman Bel Geddes, Aline Bernstein, Jo Mielziner, and *Ill. 238* Boris Aronson. An important figure in the early days was Robert Edmond Jones who through his connection with the Provincetown *Ills. 236, 243* Players was instrumental in furthering the career of the United States' first outstanding playwright, Eugene O'Neill. O'Neill, who was the son of a romantic actor, was profoundly influenced by Strindberg, and also by his early seafaring life. This provided him with material for many of the plays which shocked the complacency of contemporary audiences, and startled them into awareness of a world not yet explored by American writers. O'Neill, who was equally at home with Greek drama, realism, symbolism and expres- *Ills. 236, 243* sionism, stands at present as the main contribution of the United States to the history of world drama.

There was no lack of good actors to interpret O'Neill, both in the United States and in London, where most of his plays have been seen and admired. But on the whole the great reputations in both countries between the wars were made in revivals of classical plays. This was particularly true of London, where work in Shakespeare's plays at the Old Vic under Lilian Baylis provided a solid foundation for the careers of many actors. Among them were Laurence Olivier, *Ill. 248* who later returned to the Old Vic as the director of England's first National Theatre company, and gave some splendid performances there; John Gielgud, a member of the Terry family, outstanding in *Ill. 245* classical parts and accounted the best Hamlet of his day; Ralph Richardson, a subtle actor of great integrity; Donald Wolfit, who toured indefatigably in Shakespeare; Michael Redgrave, a fine actor *Ill. 246* in nervous, intellectual parts, and the father of two good actresses of the next generation, Vanessa and Lynn; Anthony Quayle, who from 1948 to 1956 was an unusually youthful director of the theatre at Stratford-upon-Avon, and was succeeded by the even younger

Peter Hall; and Alec Guinness, who in the opinion of his admirers spends too much of his time in films, to the detriment of the living theatre. All these actors appeared in modern plays too. Gielgud made his West End reputation in *Richard of Bordeaux*, which brought
Ills. 246, 247 into prominence a firm of young theatre-designers, Motley, and started them on a long and successful career. But on the whole English actors owed much of their success to their training in Shakespeare, a discipline denied to the actors of the United States, who were all too often lured away by Hollywood, leaving the field clear for the actresses. An interesting exception, and one which gave much pleasure in London and New York, was the partnership between Lynn Fontanne and her husband, Alfred Lunt, who began playing together in 1924. The subtlety and sophistication of their combined talents made a success of any play they appeared in, particularly of
Ill. 244 Giraudoux's *Amphitryon 38* in translation.

The Second World War had a profound effect upon the theatre everywhere, though some of the subterranean influences which led to the final upheaval had been apparent before 1939. The dispersal of talents under Hitler, the growing dissatisfaction of theatre workers with the limitations imposed by the proscenium arch, the desire to enlarge the bounds of experience, the inadequacy of most of the new plays, created an unstable situation which needed only a sudden jolt to set the theatre off in a new direction. This was provided by the work of Bertolt Brecht, the dominating influence in the European theatre of the 1950s and 1960s.

Brecht, who first came into prominence with *The Threepenny Opera*, a modernized version of *The Beggar's Opera* with music by Kurt Weill, was for some years Reinhardt's assistant at the Deutsches Theater in Berlin, where his early plays show him attempting, in an age of experiment, to find and develop a style of his own. They foreshadow both the 'epic' theatre first adumbrated by Piscator and Brecht's own theory of 'alienation', which consists in destroying by various technical methods the theatrical illusion and so preventing the audience from becoming emotionally involved in the play. Only then, he argues, can they judge the performance and the subject-matter objectively and with intelligence.

252

It was during his exile from Germany after 1933 that Brecht, a confirmed Communist, wrote what are generally considered to be his best plays. Under their English titles these are *Mother Courage and Her Children*, *The Life of Galileo*, *The Good Woman of Setzuan*, *The Days of the Commune* and *The Caucasian Chalk Circle*. These were professionally performed after the war by the Berliner Ensemble, a company formed by Brecht at the invitation of the East German authorities and housed in the Theater am Schiffbauerdamm, where *The Threepenny Opera* had had its successful run in the 1920s. The leading lady of the troupe was Brecht's wife, Helene Weigel, who after her husband's death in 1956 continued to run the company. In that year and again in 1965 (then under the auspices of Peter

Ill. 260
Ill. 253

244 Alfred Lunt as Jupiter and his wife Lynn Fontanne as Alkmena in an adaptation by S. N. Behrman of *Amphitryon 38*, by Jean Giraudoux (1882–1944), produced in New York in 1937, and in London a year later

245 (*above*) John Gielgud, considered the finest Hamlet of his generation, in the production at the New Theatre, London, in 1934

246–7 Costume designs by Motley for (*above right*) Michael Redgrave as Antony in *Antony and Cleopatra*, and (*right*) Marius Goring as Richard III, in the 1953 season at the Royal Shakespeare Theatre, Stratford-upon-Avon

248 (*far right*) Laurence Olivier as Tattle in Congreve's *Love for Love*, revived by the National Theatre at the Old Vic, London, in its 1965 season

Daubeny's World Theatre Season) she brought her actors to London to play, in German, some of the plays already known to English audiences in translation. Among these was *The Good Woman of Setzuan*, in which Peggy Ashcroft, a leading English actress whose other outstanding parts include Hedda Gabler, had displayed incredible virtuosity in the dual roles

249 (*left*) Peggy Ashcroft with George Devine in the 1954 production of Ibsen's *Hedda Gabler* (1890) at the Lyric Theatre, Hammersmith

250 (*right*) Edith Evans as the Countess Rosmarin Ostenburg in *The Dark is Light Enough*, by Christopher Fry, at the Aldwych Theatre, London, 1954

Ill. 249

Ill. 250

of the prostitute and her male cousin. The English version of the play in which she appeared was produced at the Royal Court Theatre by George Devine, founder and director of the English Stage Company. In 1956 this group determined the future course of the English theatre with its production of John Osborne's *Look Back in Anger*. There had, immediately after the Second World War, been hopes of a revival of poetic drama in London, with the plays of T. S. Eliot and Christopher Fry. The latter saw on the stage in quick succession three of his plays, the last, *The Dark is Light Enough*, starring Edith Evans, a memorable actress who had made her name in Restoration comedy, Shaw and Wilde. But the tide of popular opinion, particularly among the younger playgoers, turned away from poetry (just as in the 1900s it had turned away from the verse-plays of Stephen Phillips) and away also from a drawing-room setting and unaccented speech in favour of the kitchen, attic, or

256

251 *Ring Round the Moon*, a translation by Christopher Fry of *L'Invitation au Château*, by Jean Anouilh, produced by Peter Brook at the Globe Theatre, London, in 1950, with Paul Scofield and Claire Bloom (*centre*), Margaret Rutherford and Daphne Newton (*stage right*). Décor by Oliver Messel

bedsitting-room and the accents of the semi-educated. Typical of these new plays, which dispensed with the need for over-elaborate sets or costumes, were Wesker's *Roots* and *The Kitchen*, Pinter's *The Caretaker*, and Ann Jellicoe's *The Knack*.

The innovations introduced into his plays by Brecht, and his insistence that the actor must not attempt to 'become' the character which he is portraying – in direct contradiction to the 'method' of Stanislavsky – led to a new style of acting and production, which has been particularly influential in the emergent theatres of eastern Europe. In the English theatre Brecht's influence has been very marked, not only in the current style of producing Shakespeare and other classical plays, but in such new works as Bolt's *A Man For All*

252 The last scene in *Macbeth* in the 1967 production at the Royal Shakespeare Theatre, directed by Peter Hall, and designed by John Bury, the costumes in collaboration with Ann Curtis. Paul Scofield (*see Ill. 251*) played Macbeth and

Vivien Merchant Lady Macbeth. This production was taken to Moscow, where it was much admired, and in January 1968 opened at the Aldwych Theatre, now the London home of the Royal Shakespeare Company

Seasons, Shaffer's *The Royal Hunt of the Sun*, John Arden's *Armstrong's Last Goodnight*, and in all the plays produced by Joan Littlewood for Theatre Workshop. At this experimental East End theatre the author's script was used as a basis for brilliant improvisation by the director, who imposed on her actors her own conception of the play. This worked well for such modern playscripts as *A Taste of Honey*, *Fings Ain't Wot They Used T'Be* and *Oh What a Lovely War*, less well for the classics. Some of Joan Littlewood's productions were seen in Paris, and her reputation stood even higher on the Continent than it did in England. Distressed by the continual drain on her resources caused by the transfer of so many of her productions to London's West End theatres, which she despised, she finally left Theatre Workshop to work as a free-lance.

A New York venture which had something in common with Theatre Workshop, The Living Theatre, under Julian Beck and his

253 The Berliner Ensemble in *The Days of the Commune* by Bertolt Brecht (1898–1956), one of the seminal influences in the theatre today. The play is a revolutionary tract presenting history in Brecht's didactic epic or ballad technique

wife Judith Malina, has had an equally chequered career, and after a theatrically successful but financially unrewarding series of experimental plays the group took refuge in West Berlin. Meanwhile, the European theatre, as so often before, has been strongly influenced by new ideas from France. The post-war theatre in Paris was largely dominated by the work of the existentialist philosopher Sartre and his contemporary Anouilh, whose plays in translation have been very *Ill. 251* popular in England. But the most important play of the 1950s was *Waiting for Godot*, by the Franco-Irish dramatist Samuel Beckett. It *Ill. 257* portrays vividly the modern obsession with human isolation. Two further manifestations of the spirit of the age have been provided by the Theatre of the Absurd and the Theatre of Cruelty. Though literary in their inception, portraying states of mind rather than of bodily activity, they have had a great influence on the staging of European plays by the demands they make both on actors and on

254 The final scene – the crucifixion – from *The Royal Hunt of the Sun*, by Peter Shaffer, at the National Theatre (Old Vic), London, in 1954, with Robert Stephens (*above*) as Atahualpa and Colin Blakely (*below*) as Pizarro

255 Costume designs by Peter Rice for *The Beaux' Stratagem*, by George Farquhar
(1678–1707), revived at the Chichester Festival Theatre in 1967. Left to right (*top
row*): Bagshot, Gibbet, and Hounslow (highwaymen), Boniface (the innkeeper)
and Squire Sullen; (*bottom row*) Foigard, Gipsy (a maid), Cherry (Boniface's
daughter) and Sir Charles Freeman

Ill. 256

directors if they are to be adequately presented. The Theatre of the
Absurd, which stems from Jarry's *Ubu Roi*, first seen in Paris as far
back as 1896, is based on the assumption that human life and endea-
vour are so essentially illogical, and language so inadequate as a
means of communication, that man's only refuge is in laughter. The
main exponent of this type of theatre is Ionesco, whose best work
has been done in such one-act plays as *The Bald Prima Donna, The*

Lesson, and *The Chairs*. The Theatre of Cruelty derives from the work of Artaud, who was connected with the surrealist movement. It is defined in his book, *Le Théâtre et son double*, published in 1938, as a theatre which acts as a catalyst and, like an outbreak of plague, frees man from the restraints of morality and reason, permitting him to return to a primitive state of ferocity and brute power. Artaud died insane. His work had a great influence in Europe, and came into England officially with the Aldwych Theatre's production of Weiss's *Persecution and Assassination of Marat as Performed by the Inmates of the Asylum of Charenton under the Direction of the Marquis de Sade*, known briefly as *The Marat/Sade*. The effect of the Theatre of Cruelty on English playwrights is difficult to assess as yet, but it probably counted for something in the savageries of Rudkin's *Afore Night*

256 The Theatre of the Absurd: a sketch by David Hockney for Alfred Jarry's *Ubu Roi*, first produced in Paris in 1896 and revived at the Royal Court Theatre in London in 1966. Hockney's décor and costumes set the monstrous figure of Père Ubu in a landscape of Pop Art

Comes, where a farm-labourer is decapitated and torn in pieces, and in the stoning of a baby in its pram in Bond's *Saved*. The protests which greeted the first productions of Ibsen's plays were heard again after the first nights of both these plays, and will probably prove just as ineffectual.

The most recent innovation in the theatre is the Theatre of Fact, which appears to derive basically from the Living Newspaper technique popular in the United States in the 1930s. Material dealing with recent historical events like the assassination of President Kennedy or the war in Vietnam is taken bodily from official sources and put on with as little arrangement as possible. This appears to be the negation of art, and it will be interesting to see what further progress in the development of the non- or anti-play will be made next.

The *avant-garde* theatre of realism has given way to the *avant-garde* theatre of man's predicament in a hostile environment. Meanwhile,

257 Samuel Beckett's *Waiting for Godot*, first performed in Paris in 1953 and produced in London by Peter Hall at the Arts Theatre in 1955

there are less publicized but equally significant activities going on in all countries. On the technical side the most important figure in the French theatre, apart from Barrault, has undoubtedly been Jean Vilar, founder of the Théâtre National Populaire, whose efforts to secure a vast working-class audience for good plays, old and new, was greatly helped by the decentralization of the French theatre consequent on the formation of regional theatre centres throughout the country. One of the most important, at Villeurbanne, is run by Roger Planchon, generally recognized as one of the most stimulating directors working in the French theatre today.

The draining-away of theatrical talent from Germany before the war, and the subsequent partition of the country, seems to have had a paralyzing effect upon her playwrights, though materially the theatre flourishes. More new theatres were built in Germany after the war than anywhere else in Europe, most of them in a contemporary architectural idiom, and extremely well equipped. The best German-language plays of recent years have come from two playwrights resident in Switzerland, Max Frisch and Friedrich Dürrenmatt. Italy has produced Ugo Betti and Eduardo de Filippo, who with his brother Peppino has done much to keep alive the Neapolitan tradition of farce-playing. Soviet Russia has not yet produced an outstanding playwright, though several Soviet plays have been successful in England, among them three by Arbuzov.

In the United States an interesting phenomenon of recent years has been the success of several small experimental theatres off-Broadway, where the early plays of Edward Albee, an outstanding *Ill. 258* new writer, were first seen. A great advance has also been made in the rapid development of theatre outside New York, in connection with work in the universities, whose drama departments often run theatres comparable to European civic or repertory ones. The most impressive contribution of the United States to the history of the modern theatre, however, is found in the field of the 'musical'. The early musical comedies popularized in London by George Edwardes, which later gave way to the light musical plays of Ivor Novello, turned in New York towards the integrated song-and-dance shows, often based on an existing work, which mingled good music, a strong plot, professional dancing and lavish scenery and costumes to

Ill. 259 produce such world-wide successes as *Oklahoma!*, *My Fair Lady* (based on Shaw's *Pygmalion*) and *West Side Story*. The influence of these and other American spectacles has resulted in a raising of standards all round, noticeable in England in such works as Lionel Bart's *Oliver!* (based on Dickens' *Oliver Twist*).

Apart from changes in subject-matter and acting styles, the most significant development in the modern theatre has been the jettison-ing of the proscenium arch and the front curtain. This is apparent

Ill. 260 in such diverse buildings as the Mermaid Theatre in London, the Chichester Festival Theatre, the Stratford, Ontario, Shakespearean

Ill. 261 Festival Theatre, and the Arena Stage, Washington, D.C. The open platform stages of the first three derive from the early European and Elizabethan stages; the theatre-in-the-round at Washington from an even more primitive form of theatre. It has been introduced into England, but has as yet made little headway in the more conservative centres. But the abolition of the front curtain, sometimes with an

258 Uta Hagen, George Grizzard and Arthur Hill in *Who's Afraid of Virginia Woolf?* by Edward Albee, first produced in New York in 1962 and in London, also with Uta Hagen, in 1964

259 The Ascot Scene from *My Fair Lady*, based on Shaw's *Pygmalion*, and one of the most successful musicals ever written. Lyrics by Alan Jay Lerner, music by Frederick Loewe, produced at the Mark Hellinger Theatre, New York, in 1956 and at Drury Lane in 1958. Costumes by Cecil Beaton and scenery by Oliver Smith

apron stage built out beyond the proscenium arch, has become standard practice at the Stratford-upon-Avon and National Theatres, and in such commercial theatres as pride themselves on keeping up with modern developments. But until such time as new and revolutionary theatre buildings are not only designed but actually built, plays will continue to be presented on a conventional stage. Even the use of a permanent fixed set cannot alter the fact that the new plays of the 1960s are being acted in an architectural setting designed for a quite different conception of theatre. The work of scenic designers everywhere, of which Czechoslovakia has such a brilliant exponent in Josef Svoboda, may help to improve the situation a little, and meanwhile the theatre, which depends in the long run more on the actor's passion and the audience's receptivity than on any cut-and-dried method of playwriting or play presentation, will no doubt continue to flourish and form part of man's social and cultural heritage.

Ill. 262

260 The Mermaid Theatre, Puddle Dock, Blackfriars, London, built for Bernard Miles, to a design by Elidir Davies, inside the walls of an old warehouse. The open stage without proscenium arch is set for the 1960 production of *The Life of Galileo* by Bertolt Brecht

261 The Shakespearean Festival Theatre at Stratford, Ontario, 1957, has an open stage with the audience on three sides, eight acting levels and a central trap

262 A set by the Czech scene-designer Josef Svoboda for a production of Sophocles'
Oedipus the King at the Prague National Theatre, 1963. The thirty-foot wide staircase rises from the bottom of the orchestra pit, through the proscenium up to
the grid in one broad flight. The steps are semi-transparent, with the musicians
underneath, and the music was heard through perforations in the staircase

Photographic Acknowledgments

H. Acton, 235; American School of Classical Studies, Athens, 10; Apollo Theatre, 259; Bildarchiv der Österreichischen Nationalbibliothek, Vienna, 103, 109, 136, 138, 139, 140, 142, 143, 181; Brompton Studio, 126, 127, 185, 188, 193, 194, 196, 197, 198, 204, 205, 206, 207, 209, 211, 212, 213, 214, 215, 216, 217, 222, 224, 255; Francis Bruguiere, 236; Photo Bulloz, 60, 104, 108, 148, 155, 158, 162, 170, 183, 186; Central Press Agency, 229, 230; Zoe Dominic, 248; Lenare, 225; Lucca Chmel, 35; Courtauld Institute of Art, 88; G. Farnell, 1, 17; Daniel Frasnay, 240; Friedman-Abeles, 258; Photographie Giraudon, 8, 28, 33, 36, 65, 66, 67, 100, 151; Yvonne Gregory, 245; André Held, 23; Hirmer Munich, 5, 6; T. F. Holte, 252; Dr D. Kalvodová, Prague, 233, 234; Lipnitzki, 241; Angus McBean, 249, 250, 254; Mansell Collection, 15, 16, 25, 51; Mas, 92, 93; Mermaid Theatre, 260; Nationale Forschungs- und Gedenkstätten in Weimar, 144, 145, 146; Bertram Park, 219; P. Paukschta, 253; M. Rigal, 171; Royal Institute of British Architects, 262; Houston Rogers, 251, 257; Scala, 29; H. Schmidt-Glassner, 50; Edwin Smith, 24; Peter Smith, 261; Society for Cultural Relations with the USSR, 221, 223, 237; Theatermuseum Munich, 147; G. B. Wood, 34; Zumbühl Bros., 41.

Notes on the Illustrations

1 The Theatre of Dionysus in Athens.

2 Greek actor in costume holding a tragic mask, late fourth century BC. Fragment of a crater from Tarentum. Martin von Wagner Museum der Universität, Würzburg.

3 The Cart of Thespis, a reconstruction from a black-figured Attic vase-painting now in the British Museum. Dionysus, represented by his priest, on his way to the City Dionysia in a boat-shaped vehicle – the *carrus navalis* – accompanied by two flute-playing satyrs.

4 The theatre at Delphi stands in close proximity to the Temple of Apollo. This association between the two buildings is typical of the early Greek theatres, whose dramatic festivals were still part of a religious ceremony.

5 Clytemnestra killing Cassandra, from a red-figured bowl from Spina by the Marlay painter, *c.* 430 BC. Museo Archeologico Nazionale, Ferrara.

6 Apollo protecting Orestes from the Furies, an early Apulian volute crater from Ruvo, *c.* 370. In the final section of the *Oresteia* Orestes takes refuge in the sanctuary of Apollo at Delphi (*see Ill. 4*). Museo Nazionale Archeologico, Naples.

7 Actors dressed as birds, *c.* 500 BC, from a black-figured œnochoe. British Museum.

8 Hellenistic statuette of a comic actor wearing a mask, from Tralles in Turkey. This is interesting as showing the actor's face inside his mask, and also the crossed feet and clasped hands, a characteristic attitude shown in many portrayals of comic actors. Istanbul Museum.

9 Archaic Punic comic mask from Tunis, unpainted. Musée du Bardo, Tunisia.

10 Hellenistic comic mask. Museum, Athens.

11 Roman marble mask of a tragic heroine. Museo Nazionale Archeologico, Naples.

12 Actor in Old Comedy, mid-fourth century BC, terracotta statuette from the Piraeus. British Museum.

13 Actors in Old Comedy, mid-fourth century BC, terracotta statuettes. Staatliche Museen, Berlin.

14 The restored theatre at Epidaurus. This theatre, which is acoustically perfect, is used every year for a summer festival of classical Greek plays, and also for verse-speaking contests by children from near-by schools.

15 Menander in his studio with New Comedy masks, marble relief. Lateran Museum, Rome.

16 A scene from a Roman comedy, wall-painting from the House of Casca in Pompeii, before AD 79.

17 The Roman theatre at Sabratha in North Africa.

18–19 Actors in New Comedy, terracotta statuettes. The one on the left wears a short tunic and cloak (*sagulum*), the other a short tunic, with the longer woollen cloak used for travelling. British Museum.

20 A scene from Terence's *Adelphi*, from the *Codex Vaticanus*, a ninth-century copy by Adelricus of the fourth- or fifth-century original, now in the Vatican Museum. Compare the door on the extreme left with that in *Ill. 22*. The originals were done while the plays were still being performed and may therefore be taken as evidence for Roman stagecraft and costumes.

21 A Roman mime play, a reconstruction by Cube of a wall-painting in Pompeii, before AD 79.

22 A miser protecting his treasure from thieves, a vase-painting by Assteas, 360–330 BC, found at Nola in Italy. Staatliche Museen, Berlin.

23 Tragic actor, wall-painting from Herculaneum, before AD 79.

24 'Bikini'-clad girls, late third century AD, mosaic in the Piazza Armerina, Sicily.

25 Roman masks of a slave and a flute-player, mosaic. They much resemble those shown on a marble relief now in Naples, where an irate father confronts his drunken son, who is accompanied by just such a slave and flute-girl as in Menander's *Epitrepontes*. Capitoline Museum, Rome.

26 Medieval entertainers in fools' dress, from the manuscript of *Li Romans d'Alixandre*, written and illuminated in Flanders *c.* 1340. Bodleian Library, Oxford (264, f.84v), courtesy the Curators of the Bodleian Library.

27 A medieval glove-puppet booth, also from *Li Romans d'Alixandre* (f. 54v). It bears a striking resemblance to the modern Punch-and-Judy booth. Courtesy the Curators of the Bodleian Library, Oxford.

28 A play by Terence being read and mimed, the frontispiece to the illuminated *Terence des Ducs*, *c.* 1400, Bibliothèque de l'Arsenal, Paris (MS. Cod. Lat. Ars. 664). Calliopius, in a small central booth, is reading, or reciting, one of Terence's plays while four masked actors mime it to music. There is a very similar illustration in a Terence Codex in the Bibliothèque National (Cod. Lat. 7907a).

29 The Empress Theodora, mosaic from San Vitale, Ravenna, *c.* 545. She became Empress in AD 527, and may have encouraged the performance in Byzantium of religious plays which preserved something of the classical traditions of acting and stagecraft for later ages.

30 The Three Marys at the Tomb, from the Benedictional of Robert of Jumièges, *c.* 980. The leading Mary is carrying a censer and perhaps an incense boat. It is interesting to compare the token sepulchre on which the Angel of the Resurrection is seated in church with the practicable oblong sarcophagus in *Ill. 34*, and the one in which the body of the actor playing Christ is being deposited on the extreme right-hand side of *Ill. 42*. Bibliothèque Publique, Rouen.

31 The Easter *trope* 'Quem quaeritis?', from a fourteenth-century Sarum Processional, formerly in the possession of the Church of St John the Evangelist, Dublin, now in the Bodleian Library, Oxford (Rawlinson Liturg. MS. D.4). Courtesy the Curators of the Bodleian Library.

32 An alabaster plaque of the Resurrection, from Nottingham. The Resurrection, a favourite subject with medieval artists, was never portrayed in Byzantine art, and it is likely that this scene was directly inspired by the liturgical drama. Victoria and Albert Museum, London.

33 *Le Martyre de S. Apolline, c.* 1460, by Jehan Fouquet (1415–83). The brutal realism of the scene contrasts with the reticence of Greek tragedy, where acts of violence were never shown on stage. Musée Condé, Chantilly.

34 Three scenes from the life of Christ, a relief on the West front of the Chantry Chapel, St Mary's, Wakefield, Yorkshire.

35 Christ driving out the money-changers from the Temple, carving by Master Wilhelm Rollinger on a choir stall (destroyed in the Second World War) in St Stephen's Church, Vienna.

36 The Valenciennes Passion Play, 1547, manuscript by Hubert Cailleau. Bibliothèque Nationale (MS. 12536 f. 2v).

37 The Triumph of Isabella, Brussels, 1615, by Denis van Alsloot. In the procession Biblical and mythological scenes follow each other closely. These give some idea of the way in which Biblical scenes may have been acted on perambulating carts, a method particularly favoured in medieval England. Victoria and Albert Museum, London.

38 Christ's Descent into Hell. School of Hieronymus Bosch, first quarter of the sixteenth century. Metropolitan Museum of Art, New York (Harris Brisbane Dick Fund, 1926).

39 Devil's mask from the Tyrol. The devils, who were always comic, were probably played by the ambulant entertainers shown in *Ill. 26*. Their animal masks are found later in the Italian popular comedy. Tiroler Volkskunstmuseum, Innsbruck.

40 The Three Wise Men, from a sixteenth-century Flemish Nativity play. Collection Mr Ifan Kyrle Fletcher, London.

41 Two medieval devils by Jakob Ruoff (copyist Wolfgang Haller), from the manuscript of the *Weingartenspiel*, Zurich,

1539. Vadiana Stadtbibliothek, St Gallen.

42 Scenes from the Valenciennes Passion Play, 1547. From the same manuscript as *Ill. 36* Bibliothèque Nationale, Paris.

43 A scene from *Maître Pierre Pathelin, c.* 1465, a woodcut from an edition published *c.* 1500.

44 A farce performed during a sixteenth-century country fair, detail from a painting by Pieter Balten (died 1598). Rijksmuseum, Amsterdam.

45–9 Terence on the Renaissance stage. Four woodcuts from the Trechsel edition of Terence's plays (Lyons, 1493), one (*Ill. 49*) from the Venice edition of 1497. 45 An academic audience waits for the performance. What can be seen of the pillared and curtained stage, evidently erected in an upper room for the occasion, is very like that for the *Andria* (*Ill. 49*) and the *Eunuchus* (*Ill. 48*).

46 Calliopius speaks the prologue to the *Heauton Timorumenos*.

47 A scene from the *Adelphi*.

48 A scene from the *Eunuchus*.

49 A scene from the *Andria*. The numerous 'houses' of the medieval stage have been reduced to four, in imitation of the classical setting of doors set in a back wall, an interesting mingling of classical and medieval practices. The whole stage stands on a platform mounted on trestles, rather like the *phlyakes* stage in *Ill. 22*, or the *commedia dell'arte* stage in *Ill. 68*.

50 The stage and auditorium of the Teatro Olimpico, Vicenza, 1580–4. From *The Baroque Theatre*, Margarete Baur-Heinhold.

51 The auditorium of the Teatro Farnese, Parma, 1618–19, which was badly damaged during the Second World War. Its side wings and backcloth inaugurated a style which persisted until the end of the nineteenth century, and is still

used for opera and ballet in many of the great theatres of the world.

52 Design for stage-set by one of the Bibiena family. The exploitation by the younger Bibienas of the *scena d'angolo* opened up new vistas in European scene design. Drawing from the Yordini Collection, Milan.

53–5 Three stage settings from the section of *Architettura* (by Sebastiano Serlio, 1475–1554) dealing with perspective, published in Venice in 1545. It was translated into English in 1611. The sets, in symmetrical perspective, are intended for a temporary stage erected in a large hall.

56 Costume design by Stefano della Bella (1610–64). Victoria and Albert Museum, London.

57 Costume design by Henri Gissey (1621–73). The marginal notes give the original colours.

58–9 Costume designs by Lodovico Burnacini (1636–1707), probably intended for a Court performance in Vienna, from the Nationalbibliothek there. They show strongly the influence of the *commedia dell'arte*, and were probably intended for a *zanni*, possibly Harlequin.

60 A *commedia dell'arte* troupe at the Court of Henry of Navarre, c. 1578–90, by François Bunel the Younger. This painting is very similar to a sixteenth-century one in Stockholm, attributed to Franz Porbus, probably because such a scene appeared frequently in *commedia dell'arte* scenarios (*see also Ill. 96*). Musée de Béziers.

61 Pantalone serenading Donna Lucia, a painting c. 1580 by an unknown artist. Perhaps the servant with the book on the far right is doing the actual serenading. (For other illustrations of Pantalone see *Ills. 60, 63, 67, 96*.) Drottningholm Theatre Museum.

62 Coviello, a drawing from Francesco Bertelli's *Il carnevale*

italiano mascherato, Venice, 1642.

63 Pantalone, an engraving by Jacques Callot, 1618. A Venetian, he wears a red woollen cap and red velvet suit, with a loose black cloak, and Turkish slippers.

64 Il Capitano, in Venetian glass from Murano, second half of the sixteenth century. This braggart soldier is the prototype of Shakespeare's Ancient Pistol. For a later French version, see the figure far left in *Ill. 99*. Kunsthistorisches Museum, Vienna.

65 Arlequin, by Dolivar after Le Pautre, seventeenth century. He is wearing his original cat mask and carrying a *bat*, but his loose patched costume has become a well-fitting suit of brilliantly coloured silk diamonds. Cabinet des Estampes, Bibliothèque Nationale, Paris.

66 *Commedia dell'arte* masks. They resemble the half-mask worn by Harlequin (*see Ill. 65*), which left the mouth free, and are also reminiscent of some known to have been worn by Neapolitan Pulcinellas. Bibliothèque de l'Arsenal, Paris.

67 A *commedia dell'arte* troupe, c. 1580, with Isabella Andreini (1562–1604), the best-known actress of the *commedia dell'arte*, who gave her name to the heroines of innumerable scenarios. Musée Carnavalet, Paris.

68 Razullo and Cucurucu, from Callot's *I Balli di Sfessania* (a series of engravings of stock characters in the *commedia dell'arte*), published in 1621.

69 Pulcinella, engraving by Johann Georg Puschner from G. Lambranzi's *Deliciae Theatrales* (The New and Curious School of Theatrical Dancing), 1716.

70 An open-air performance of an Italian comedy, Verona, 1772. An oil-painting by Marco Marcola. It would be tempting to attribute the play to Goldoni, but it represents what must have been a stock situation in

many of the *commedia dell'arte* scenarios. Art Institute of Chicago (the gift of Emily Crane Chadbourne). Courtesy of the Art Institue of Chicago.

71 A scene from the *Interlude of the Four Cardinal Virtues* (Temperance, Justice, Prudence and Fortitude, who, with Wilful, make up the cast); a woodcut of c. 1547. British Museum.

72 Edward Alleyn, a portrait by an unknown artist at Dulwich College, which Alleyn founded after his retirement from the stage as the College of God's Gift. He was the chief actor of the Admiral's Men, and the first to play many of Marlowe's heroes, including Tamburlaine, Doctor Faustus (*see Ill. 84*) and Barabas in *The Jew of Malta*. Reproduced by permission of the Governors of Dulwich College.

73 Richard Burbage – traditionally a self-portrait. Burbage, whose father built the first theatre in London in 1576, was the leading actor of the Lord Chamberlain's Men (later the King's Men), and the first to play many of Shakespeare's heroes, including Hamlet, Lear, Othello and Richard III. Reproduced by permission of the Governors of Dulwich College.

74 Reconstruction of an Elizabethan theatre of c. 1580–90, perhaps that built by James Burbage in 1576, by C. Walter Hodges (*The Globe Restored*, Ernest Benn Ltd, 1953, p. 73). The auditorium shows the influence of the innyard and the bear-pit, but the stage owes its Baroque façade more to the influence of Flemish theatres and triumphal arches (*see Ills. 76, 77*), combined with the curtained booth of the stages shown in *Ills. 44, 68*.

75 The Swan Theatre, c. 1596, copy by Arend van Buchel of Utrecht of a drawing sent to him by his friend Johannes de Witt during a visit to London. It helps to confirm evidence

drawn from other sources, particularly as regards the large open stage, the stage building with its pillars and flag, and the three galleries for spectators. Library of the University of Utrecht.

76 A Rederijkers stage at Antwerp, 1561, with a *platea* in front of a two-storey building and a curtained window above a central curtained opening. Such stages were built for the members of Flemish Chambers of Rhetoric for civic entertainments; they may have been known to James Burbage when he built his Theatre in London in 1576. Bibliothèque Royale, Brussels.

77 A triumphal arch for the Coronation of James I, 1603 – The Flemish Arch – from Stephen Harrison's *Arches of Triumph*, 1604. This shows clearly the influence of the Antwerp stage (*Ill. 76*). In some of the arches there were niches for the accommodation of living actors (the London arch had an actor representing the Thames, and Alleyn as the Genius of the City).

78 The exterior of the Globe Theatre, from Visscher's *View of London*, Amsterdam, 1616. This octagonal building probably represents the second Globe, built in 1614. The first Globe, shown on Norden's map of 1600, appears to be circular, and is so shown on an engraving by Hollar of 1644. The flag and the presence of people àt the door seem to indicate that a play is in progress.

79 A Cambridge students' performance of *Roxana*, by William Alabaster (1567–1640), detail from the frontispiece of an edition of 1632. The temporary stage has a background of curtains, which resemble those of the Terence and *commedia dell'arte* stages rather than the solid architecture of the public theatres in London.

80 William Shakespeare (1546–1616), the so-called 'Chandos' portrait. It appears to be a slightly later romanticized version of the engraving by Martin Droeshout which forms the frontispiece to the First Folio of 1623. National Portrait Gallery, London.

81 Characters in *Titus Andronicus*, believed to have been drawn by Henry Peachum, in 1595, from a manuscript at Longleat. Reproduced by courtesy of the Marquess of Bath.

82 Richard Tarleton, from an initial letter in a manuscript by John Scottowe. Tarleton was an excellent extempore actor – which may have called forth Shakespeare's rebuke to the clown in *Hamlet* (*see p. 81*). Several of Shakespeare's comic characters, among them the Gravedigger in *Hamlet*, appear to be based on his memories of Tarleton's fooling. British Museum (Harleian MS. 3885 f. 19).

83 William Kempe, a woodcut from the title-page of his *Nine Days' Wonder*, 1600. Kempe was the chief comedian of Shakespeare's company, and is known to have been the first to play Dogberry in *Much Ado about Nothing* and Peter in *Romeo and Juliet*.

84 A scene from *The Tragical History of Doctor Faustus* by Christopher Marlowe (1564–93); a woodcut from an edition of 1636. This play was first performed by the Admiral's Men for Henslowe, with Alleyn (*see Ill. 72*) in the title role, probably between 1588 and 1592. Mephistopheles, whose costume is reminiscent of that of the devils in the liturgical play (*see Ill. 41*) is appearing through the trapdoor with which Elizabethan theatres are known to have been equipped, in response to the conjurations of Faustus, safely enclosed within his magic circle.

85 The second Blackfriars

Theatre, built by James Burbage on the site now occupied by the offices of *The Times*. (The first theatre, used from 1576 to 1584 by the Children of the Chapel Royal and St Paul's and Oxford's Boys – the 'little eyases' mentioned in *Hamlet* II. 2 – was in a different part of the building.) Reconstruction by the late J. H. Farrar. Reproduced by permission of the Architect of the Greater London Council.

86–7 Costume designs by Inigo Jones (1573–1652) for two masks given at Whitehall in 1609 and 1611, both with texts by Ben Jonson (1571–1638). They are in the Roman style, and show Continental, particularly Flemish, influence. Although these costumes were not designed for the public theatre, it is reasonable to suppose that they approximate roughly to what Shakespeare's audiences would have expected to see. Devonshire Collection, Chatsworth. Reproduced by permission of the Trustees of the Chatsworth Settlement.

88 Inigo Jones' Tragic Scene, which closely resembles that of Serlio (*Ill. 54*). Devonshire Collection, Chatsworth. Reproduced by permission of the Trustees of the Chatsworth Settlement.

89 The frontispiece to Francis Kirkman's *The Wits; or, Sport upon Sport*, 1673. The gallery at the back of the platform stage with spectators in it seems to confirm the presence of such a feature in the Swan Theatre (*see Ill. 75*). The great importance of this illustration lies in the evidence it provides for the lighting of the stage by overhead chandeliers and footlights. For similar lighting in France see *Ill. 100*.

90 Itinerant actors, and a platform stage, frontispiece by William Faithorne for the English translation of Paul Scarron's *Roman Comique* (1651), published in 1676.

91 Lope Felix de Vega Carpio. Many of his early plays were written for the actor-manager Jeronimo Velazquez, and may have been given at the newly opened Corral del Príncipe (*see Ill. 92*). Engraving by M.S. Larmona.

92 Reconstruction of the Corral del Príncipe, Madrid, which dates from *c.* 1582, by Juan Comba, a seventeenth-century artist. Like *Ills. 21* and *74*, it helps us to visualize the main features of the theatre it represents. Museo Municipal, Madrid.

93 A masked ball in the Teatro del Príncipe, 1766, by L.Paret. Prado, Madrid.

94 Design for a Court Theatre, *c.* 1680, attributed to Francisco Ricci. Ricci was appointed director of the Royal Theatre in the Alcázar in 1649 in the reign of Philip IV, and died in 1685 in his seventies, in the reign of Charles II. Biblioteca Nacionale, Madrid.

95 Set designed for a revival in 1690 of *La fiera, el rayo y la piedra*, by Pedro Calderón de la Barca (1608–81). This engraving is one of twenty-four now in the Biblioteca Nacionale, Madrid. The name of the designer is not known.

96 Italian actors in France, *c.* 1577, from the *Recueil Fossard*. It may represent the Gelosi Company, which acted before Henry III at Blois in 1577 (for a somewhat similar scene see *Ill. 60*). National museum, Stockholm.

97 The simultaneous setting for *Cornélie*, by Alexandre Hardy (*c.* 1575–*c.* 1631), a design from the *Mémoire de Mahelot, Laurent et d'autres décorateurs* (MS. Bibl. Nat. Paris No. 24330, f. 30).

98 Actors in a comedy probably based on a *commedia dell'arte* scenario at the Hôtel de Bourgogne, *c.* 1630. The symmetrical architectural background and the small balustrades figure in several extant designs for this theatre (*see also Ill. 97*). Engraving by Abraham Bosse, Bibliothèque Nationale (Cabinet des Estampes), Paris.

99 The comedians of the Hôtel de Bourgogne, Turlupin, Gros-Guillaume and Gaultier-Garguille, *c.* 1630. They can be seen also in *Ills. 98* and *100*. An engraving by P.Mariette in the Bibliothèque Nationale (Cabinet des Estampes), Paris.

100 Composite painting by an unknown artist, *c.* 1670, showing comedians of the 1630s with later actors, among them Poisson (*see Ill. 150*), and Molière, first seen with his company in Paris in 1658. The setting resembles Serlio's Comic Scene (*see Ill. 53*). The chandeliers and footlights seen here are shown on an English stage in *Ill. 89*. Comédie-Française, Paris.

101–2 Engravings by Gravelot from an edition of the plays of Pierre Corneille (1606–84) published in 1764. *Le Cid (Ill. 101)*, was first produced at the Théâtre du Marais early in 1637, and is generally held to have inaugurated the great age of French classical drama. Both *Le Cid* and *Le Menteur* (*Ill. 102*) were based on Spanish originals.

103 A setting by Giacomo Torelli (1608–78) for Corneille's *Andromède*, produced at the Petit-Bourbon in 1649, and written to display the machinery and effects brought from Italy by Torelli. This design shows Perseus descending from the heavens on a winged horse to do battle with the sea-monster who is preparing to devour Andromeda (seen chained to the rocks on the stage left). Osterreichishe Nationalbibliothek, Vienna.

104 Mlle Champmeslé, leading lady of the Comédie-Française on its formation in 1680, where she played opposite Baron (*see Ill. 148*). She had previously been at the Hôtel de Bourgogne with her husband, and was the first to play many famous parts,

including Racine's Phèdre and Bérénice (*see Ill. 106*).

105–6 Engravings from an edition of the plays of Jean Racine (1639–99) published in 1676. *Ill. 105* is from *Les Plaideurs* (III, 3), first performed in 1668. *Ill. 106* is from *Bérénice*, probably the last scene, in which the lovers part because Titus, being now Emperor of Rome, cannot marry a Jewess.

107 Clowns fighting, an engraving from G. Lambranzi's *Deliciae Theatrales*, 1716 (*see also Ill. 69*). The side wings set at an angle to the stage and the arched windows appear to be painted on the backcloth.

108 Molière in Corneille's *La Mort de Pompée*, 1659, by Paul Mignard. The play was first produced in 1643 at the Théâtre du Marais. Although Molière was not considered good in tragedy, he had a great admiration for Corneille's works, and it was in *Nicomède* (first produced in 1651) that his Paris appeared in Paris in 1658 before Louis XIV. It was, however, his acting in his own farce, *Le Docteur amoureux* (now lost), that finally won the audience's approval. Comédie-Française, Paris.

109 Molière's *Le Malade Imaginaire*, Versailles, 1674, in an engraving by Le Pautre. This play was first produced at the Palais-Royal in February 1673, with Molière as the hypochondriac Argan. He died a few hours after appearing in the part for the fourth time. This posthumous production was seen at Versailles on the third day of the festivities held there in July.

110 Armande Béjart (1642–1700), wife of Molière, in the title-role of *Psyché*. The dresses worn by Armande in this lavish and very expensive production are itemized in an inventory made after Molière's death, and as this engraving by P.Brizzard is from an edition

275

of Molière's works published in 1682, it may well show her wearing one of them.

111 A scene from Molière's *Les Femmes Savantes*, an engraving from the edition of Molière's work noted above (*Ill. 110*). The set is interesting as having, behind the curtain, a recess which is reminiscent of the 'inner stage' of the Spanish and Elizabethan stage.

112 An engraving by William Dolle from the 1673 edition of *The Empress of Morocco*, a heroic drama by Elkanah Settle (1648–1724) (the Doeg of Dryden's *Absalom and Achitophel*), and the first English play to be published with scenic illustrations. It probably shows Betterton (*see Ill. 114*) and Mrs Barry.

113 Nell Gwynne (1650–87), studio of Sir Peter Lely. National Portrait Gallery, London.

114 The Closet Scene from *Hamlet* (III, 4), an engraving from Nicholas Rowe's edition of 1709. At the back are the two large portraits of the elder Hamlet and Claudius to which Hamlet refers, often replaced now by miniatures hung round the necks of Hamlet and Gertrude respectively (*see Ill. 127*). The lighting is interesting – candelabra attached to the wing by means of a batten behind.

115 Detail from a satirical print of 1731 showing John Rich (*c.* 1692–1761) as Harlequin with the Doctor and Piero, the anglicized forms of Arlecchino, Il Dottore and Pedrolino. These *commedia dell'arte* masks came into England with the 'Italian Night Scenes' imported by John Weaver (1673–1760), from which Rich developed the harlequinades that led to the development of the later English pantomime. The satire is aimed at the vogue for such ephemeral amusements as the harlequinade and *The Beggar's Opera* by John Gay, produced in 1728 with such success that

it made 'Gay rich and Rich gay'. Rich's Harlequin suit is very much like that shown in *Ill. 65*. British Museum Print Room.

116 Colley Cibber (1671–1757) as Lord Foppington in *The Relapse; or, Virtue in Danger* by Sir John Vanbrugh (1664–1726). This was first produced at Drury Lane in 1696, and in 1777 was rewritten by Sheridan as *A Trip to Scarborough*. Cibber is now chiefly remembered for his *Apology*, 1740, which contains some admirable descriptions of Restoration acting. An engraving by J. Simon after Grisoni's portrait.

117 The interior of the Regency Theatre, London, as it was in 1817, an engraving from Robert Wilkinson's *Theatrum Illustrata*, 1825. After a chequered career and many changes of name the theatre was taken over by the Bancrofts (*see Ill. 210*) and became famous as the Prince of Wales's.

118 The exterior of the Tankard Street Theatre, Ipswich, an engraving from Wilkinson's *Theatrum Illustrata*, 1825. Here David Garrick (*see Ill. 119*) made his first professional appearance in 1741 under the name of Lyddal, playing Aboan in *Oroonoko*, by Thomas Southerne (1660–1746), first performed at Drury Lane in 1695.

119 David Garrick (1717–97) and his wife Eva Maria Viegel (1724–1822), a portrait by William Hogarth. Reproduced by gracious permission of Her Majesty the Queen.

120 A 'cut-out' scene by Philip James de Loutherbourg (1740–1812). Having studied in Paris and Italy, he made important reforms at Drury Lane in lighting effects and scenery, and by putting lights behind the proscenium arch helped to confine the actors within the 'picture-frame' to the added detriment of the already attenuated forestage. Victoria and Albert Museum, London.

121 Peg Woffington (*c.* 1714–60) as Mistress Ford in *The Merry Wives of Windsor*, after a portrait by E. Haytley, 1751. Excellent in comedy, though not in tragedy, she became the rage of London when in 1740 she appeared as Sir Harry Wildair in *The Constant Couple* by George Farquhar (1678–1707). British Museum.

122 Kitty Clive (*née* Catherine Raftor, 1711–85), as Isabella in *The Old Debauchees*, by Henry Fielding (1707–54), first produced at Drury Lane in 1732; an engraving of 1750, when the play may have been revived. She was at her best in low comedy and burlesque.

123 Charles Macklin (*c.* 1700–97) as Shylock, in an engraving by Nutter after Boyne. He first played the part on 14 February 1741, making the character dignified and tragic instead of comic.

124 A scene from *She Stoops to Conquer* by Oliver Goldsmith (1730–74). Engraving by W. Humphrey after a painting by Parkinson.

125 The Screen Scene from *The School for Scandal*, by Richard Brinsley Sheridan (1751–1816), an engraving of 1778. The first production took place at Drury Lane on 8 May 1777. Characteristic of the period are the painted backcloth and wings, the large forestage, and the boxes directly rising from it (*see also Ill. 117*).

126 Anglers outside Sadler's Wells Theatre, 1796, a drawing by George Cruikshank. Victoria and Albert Museum, London.

127 William Henry West Betty (1791–1874), a child prodigy known as Master Betty or 'The Young Roscius', who at the age of thirteen astonished London audiences with his acting in the great tragic roles of Shakespeare, here seen as Hamlet. Betty, who was also much admired as Young Norval in *Douglas* by the Rev. John

Home (1722–1808), had a spectacular career for a few years, but passed the rest of his long life in obscurity.

128 James Quin in the title-role of *Coriolanus* by James Thomson (1700–48), Covent Garden, January 1749, with Peg Woffington and George Anne Bellamy (*c.* 1727–88). This shows the final and somewhat eccentric development of the seventeenth-century Roman kilt, and the anachronistic costumes of the women, wearing the Elizabethan head-dress usually associated with Mary Queen of Scots. Burney Collection, British Museum Print Room.

129 A German Fool (*Narr*), end of the fifteenth century, an engraving by Crispinus Passaeus from George Wither's *Emblems*, 1635. His costume is reminiscent of that of the medieval fool (*see Ill. 26*), and persisted for a long time, Shakespeare's Touchstone, for instance, being very often dressed in a similar hooded head-dress with bells. Bodleian Library, Oxford (Douce Portfolio 142, f. 66, no. 68). Courtesy the Curators of the Bodleian Library.

130–1 An open-air stage, woodcuts from a 1574 edition of *Kinderzucht* by Johann Rasser.

132 A woodcut from the title-page of *Der Teufel lässt keinen Landsknecht mehr in die Hölle fahren* by Hans Sachs, probably produced in the Marthakirche, Nuremberg. The devil's costume resembles that of Mephistopheles in Marlowe's *Doctor Faustus* (*see Ill. 84*). The title of the play is a pun, *Hölle* meaning hell and the hot space behind the large porcelain stove up which the devil is climbing.

133 The mastersinger Hans Sachs, whose dramatic activity began about 1518, an engraving by Jost Amman.

134 A seventeenth-century German stage, title-page engraving from *Teutsche Schaubühne*, 1655, by I. Clauss.

135 John Goodwin as Hanswurst, or, as the German title of the picture has it: '*Der kurtzweillige Hanswurst aus Engelland Johann Guttwen*'. British Museum Print Room (1933, 10, 14, 415).

136 *Pietas Victrix,* by Nicolaus Avancinus (1612–86), one of nine illustrations from an edition published in 1659, the year in which the play was staged in Vienna with all the latest scenery and mechanical devices imported from Italy. Plays of this kind were common in Jesuit schools all over Europe, and served to train the pupils in declamation, singing and movement as well as in Latin, the language in which they were written, while the use of Italian scenery spread from such productions to the Court and so to the public theatres everywhere.

137 Johann Christoph Gottsched and his wife, a portrait by an unknown artist. The modern German theatre is usually considered to have evolved from the collaboration of Gottsched and Carolina Neuber (*Ill. 138*). Of Gottsched's own plays *Der sterbende Cato* (1732), based partly on the *Cato* (1713) of Joseph Addison (1672–1719), was the most successful, in spite of his efforts to costume it in correct Roman style, an innovation too far in advance of the time.

138 Carolina Neuber as Elizabeth I in Thomas Corneille's *Essex*, an engraving after von Hausmann.

139 Actors preparing for a *Haupt- und Staatsaktion* in Nuremberg, *c.* 1730; an engraving by P. Decker. It is interesting to compare the costume of the plumed and kilted hero with that of Quin in *Coriolanus* (*see Ill. 128*). It is not known what play the actors are about to perform,

but it represents the type of popular drama against which Gottsched and Carolina Neuber reacted by producing austere translations of French neo-classical plays of the seventeenth century.

140 Friedrich Schröder as Falstaff, 1780, an engraving by Pippo. Schröder was the leading actor of the German stage from *c.* 1771 to his retirement in 1798. In his first production of *Hamlet* he played the Ghost to Brockmann's Hamlet (*see Ill. 142*), and after playing Laertes and the Gravedigger in subsequent productions he finally appeared in the title-role.

141 Johann Wolfgang Goethe, a portrait by Georg Oswald, 1799.

142 Johann Brockmann (1745–1812) as Hamlet in a production in Berlin in 1778, by the company of Karl Döbbelin (1727–93). After an engraving by Daniel Chodowiecky. Döbbelin, who started his acting career in the company of Carolina Neuber (*see Ill. 138*), played the Ghost in this production, and his daughter Caroline was the Ophelia.

143 The interior of the first Burgtheater in Vienna, from an engraving in the Vienna State Museum. It stood until 1888. After its demolition a new Burgtheater was built on the Franzensring, and rebuilt after severe damage in the Second World War.

144 Goethe (*see Ill. 141*) as Orestes with Corona Schroeter as Iphigenia, 1779, in Goethe's *Iphigenie auf Tauris,* a painting by G. M. Kraus.

145 The Court Theatre at Weimar during the directorship of Goethe (*see Ill. 141*), water-colour.

146 Friedrich von Schiller, a portrait by Anton Graff.

147 Act V, scene 12 of *Die Verschwörung des Fiesko zu Genua* by Schiller, at the Court Theatre, Weimar, in *c.* 1810.

The play deals with the conspiracy of Fiesko against the ruling family of Genoa, during which he accidentally kills his young wife, Leonore. The conspirators, in tragic cloaks and plumed hats, surround the despairing Fiesko and the expiring Leonore. On the stage left are two conspirators watching the tragedy in an attitude which strongly resembles the usual nineteenth-century pose of Hamlet and Horatio watching the funeral of Ophelia. Theatermuseum, Munich.

148 Michel Baron, a portrait by Rigaud. Trained by Molière, on whose death he joined the rival company at the Hôtel de Bourgogne, where he played the young heroes of Racine. He became the leading man of the Comédie-Française in the formation by Louis XIV in 1680. Perpignan Museum.

149 Giuseppe Biancolelli, known as Dominique, a portrait by an unknown artist of the seventeenth-century French school. Museum of La Scala, Milan.

150 Raymond Poisson as Crispin, an engraving by G. Edelinck after a painting by Netscher. The part of Crispin is first found in *L'Ecolier de Salamanque* (1654) by Paul Scarron (1610–60) (*see also Ill. 90*), but it was Poisson who made it popular, introducing it into several of his own plays. After his death it was played by his son and grandson, and then passed to Préville (*Ill. 162*). Kongelige Bibliotek, Copenhagen.

151 Actors of the Comédie-Italienne, Paris, a painting by Nicolas Lancret. The central figure is Scapin, who plays a large part in the comedies of Molière, and grouped round him are Silvie, Mezzetin, Gille, Harlequin, Columbine and Il Dottore. Louvre, Paris.

152 The Italian actors banished from Paris in 1697 on the orders of Louis XIV, an engraving by L. Jacob after Watteau. Col-

umbine (*centre*) is the daughter of Dominique (*Ill. 149*). It was not until 1716 that an Italian company returned to Paris, under the leadership of Luigi Riccoboni (*c.* 1675–1753), known as Lelio. British Museum Print Room.

153 A group of French actors, *c.* 1720, a detail from a painting by Watteau. The hero wears the usual plumed hat and panniered skirt. The scenery is severely classical with a painted backcloth, and probably represents the courtyard of a palace, forming a permanent set for the entire play. Metropolitan Museum of Art, New York.

154 Actors at the Foire Saint-Laurent, *c.* 1720. They probably represent (from stage right to left) the *confidante*, the hero, the heroine, and the villain, in a romantic comedy. An engraving from *Foire Saint-Laurent*, A. Heulhard, 1878.

155 Theatre at the Foire Saint-Laurent, 1721, destroyed 1761. This painting shows Arlequin and his companions on the balcony which, unlike that in *Ill. 154*, is raised well above the crowd, parading before appearing in a farce based probably on a *commedia dell'arte* scenario. Musée Carnavalet, Paris.

156 A scene from *Sémiramis* by Voltaire (1694–1778) at the Comédie-Française in 1748. Drawing by G. de Saint-Aubin. The setting for this play was designed by the Slotdz brothers, and is reminiscent of that shown in *Ill. 153*. Private Collection.

157 Adrienne Lecouvreur in Corneille's *La Mort de Pompée*. From *Costumes et Annales des Théâtres de Paris*, vol. IV, 1788–9.

158 Henri-Louis Lekain, portrait by S.-B. Lenoir. Comédie-Française, Paris.

159 The 'apotheosis' of Voltaire on 30 March 1778, at the Comédie-Française, an engraving after Moreau le Jeune. It is interesting to compare this theatre with Drury Lane during

The School for Scandal, produced a year earlier (*see Ill. 125*).

160 A scene from *L'Orphelin de la Chine*, produced in 1777, from an illustrated edition of Voltaire's plays published in 1883–5.

161 A scene from *Le Barbier de Séville* (1775) by Pierre-Augustin Caron de Beaumarchais (1732–99). Contemporary pen-and-ink sketch. Collection Rondel, Bibliothèque de l'Arsenal, Paris.

162 The actor Préville as Mezzetin, a portrait by Van Loo. Comédie-Française, Paris.

163 A scene from Beaumarchais's *Le Mariage de Figaro* (1784) in an engraving attributed to Moreau le Jeune.

164 A stage-set in diagonal perspective by Jean-Nicolas Servandony (Giovanni Niccolò Servandoni). Pen drawing. Albertina, Vienna.

165 A stage-set by Louis-René Boquet (*fl.* 1760–82). Probably intended for a ballet, it is in marked contrast to the solidity and severity of the work of such designers as Servandony (*Ill. 164*). Bibliothèque de l'Opera, Paris.

166 The eighteenth-century Dock Street Theatre in Charleston, South Carolina, the second to be built on the site. It was one of the earliest theatres in the American colonies. On stage is a setting of houses in perspective which seems to derive indirectly from Serlio's Comic Scene (*see Ill. 53*), and over the proscenium arch are the Royal Arms of England. Theatre Collection, Harvard University.

167 The Screen Scene from Sheridan's *The School for Scandal*, probably at the Park Theatre, New York, *c.* 1802. Painting by William Dunlap. Theatre Collection, Harvard University.

168 The Chestnut Street Theatre, Philadelphia, Pa., built in 1793 on the plans of the Theatre Royal at Bath. It was burnt down in 1856.

169 Helena Modjeska, formerly Modrzejewska. She made her last appearance at the Metropolitan Opera House, New York, in 1905.

170 François-Joseph Talma, the pupil of Molé (*Ill. 161*), and later acclaimed as the successor of Lekain (*Ill. 158*). A portrait in the Comédie-Française, Paris.

171 The Comédie-Française, 1808. This theatre had opened in 1790 as the Variétes-Amusantes, designed by Victor Louis (1731–1802) who made use of new materials and techniques, with wrought-iron framing replacing all timber in the roof. After some internal reconstruction, which included the installation of the large stage shown here, it reopened in 1799 as the Comédie-Française. Archives of the Comédie-Française, Paris.

172 Mrs Siddons, a sketch by George Romney. She was the leading actress of London from 1782 to her retirement in 1812, and appeared many times at Covent Garden and Drury Lane under the management of her brother John Philip Kemble. Ashmolean Museum, Oxford.

173 John Philip Kemble, a portrait by Sir Thomas Lawrence. Kemble was manager of Covent Garden during the 'Old Prices' riots, which resulted from the increase in the price of seats after rebuilding due to the fire of 1808. Guildhall Art Gallery, London.

174 Drury Lane Theatre, from Ackermann's *Microcosm of London*, 1808. The theatre was destroyed by fire in 1809 and rebuilt, re-opening in 1912.

175 A setting for any historical play, by William Capon, 1808. By permission of the Governors of the Royal Shakespeare Theatre, Stratford-upon-Avon.

176 George Frederick Cooke as Richard III, the part which he played on his first appearance at Covent Garden in 1800, probably in Colley Cibber's version. British Museum Print Room.

177 James Robinson Planché's costume design for a production of *King John* by Charles Kemble, 1824.

178 Edmund Kean as Othello, a lithograph after a painting by Lambert. Harry R. Beard Theatre Collection, Cambridge.

179 A setting for Charles Kean's production of *Richard II*, 1857. The costumes in conformity with the vogue for historical accuracy introduced by Planché (*see Ill. 177*), were based on the illuminations in a manuscript of 1319, but the scenery seems to derive more from de Loutherbourg's 'cut-outs' (*see Ill. 120*) than from Capon's careful archaeology (*see Ill. 175*). Victoria and Albert Museum, London.

180 A design by the Duke of Saxe-Meiningen for *Der Prinz von Homburg*, by Heinrich von Kleist, first performed ten years after Kleist's death. It has only comparatively recently been recognized as a masterpiece. Theatersammlung der Universität, Hamburg.

181 Ferdinand Raimund in his own play *Das Mädchen aus der Feenwelt, oder der Bauer als Millionär* (1826). Lithograph after a drawing by M. von Schwind.

182 A scene from *Der Traum ein Leben*, by Franz Grillparzer (1791–1872), based on *La vida es sueno*, by Calderón. This had scenery in a quasi-Oriental manner by Antonio de Pian (1784–1851) and costumes designed by Philipp von Stubenrauch (1784–1848). Engraving from the Theatre Collection of the Osterreichische Nationalbibliothek, Vienna.

183 The auditorium of the Comédie-Française during the first night of *Hernani* by Victor Hugo (1802–85), a painting by Albert Besnard. Victor Hugo Museum, Paris.

184 A scene from *Der böse Geist Lumpazivagabundus oder das liederliche Kleeblatt* by Johann Nestroy (1802–62), at the Theater an der Wien in 1833. Engraving from the Theatermuseum, Munich.

185 Charles Kemble and Harriet Smithson (1800–54) as Romeo and Juliet at the Odéon, Paris, 1827. Lithograph from *Souvenirs du Théâtre Anglais à Paris*, 1827. R. Eddison Collection.

186 Antoine-Louis-Prosper Lemaître (Frédérick), at Pierrefitte with Honoré de Balzac and Théophile Gautier (1811–72), a watercolour by Gautier painted in 1840 while the three friends were collaborating on a play entitled *Mercadet*. Private Collection.

187 Rachel at Covent Garden, 1841, detail of a watercolour by Lami. Enthoven Collection, Victoria and Albert Museum, London.

188 Joseph Grimaldi (1778–1837) as the Clown in *Harlequin Padmanada, or The Golden Fish*, a pantomime, probably by Charles Farley, produced at Covent Garden at Christmas 1811. Enthoven Collection, Victoria and Albert Museum, London.

189 Charles Fechter as Hamlet at the Princess's Theatre, London, 1861. Enthoven Collection, Victoria and Albert Museum, London.

190 William Macready in the title-role of *Werner* by Lord Byron, a painting by Daniel Maclise. Enthoven Collection, Victoria and Albert Museum, London.

191 Samuel Phelps as Cardinal Wolsey in Shakespeare's *Henry VIII*, a painting by Johnston Forbes-Robertson. By kind permission of the Garrick Club, London.

192 Mme Vestris and Charles Mathews the Younger in a scene from *The Conquering Game*, by William Bernard, *Duncombe's British Theatre*, vol. 35, *c*. 1865.

193 Mme Vestris and her husband in *Mr and Mrs Mathews at Home*. This was a series of vignettes in which they both played several parts, in the style of the solo performance given by the elder Charles Mathews (1776–1835). Enthoven Collection, Victoria and Albert Museum, London.

194 Edwin Booth as Richelieu, in London in 1861. Booth was seen in London again between 1880 and 1882, where he appeared at the Lyceum with Irving. Enthoven Collection, Victoria and Albert Museum, London.

195 Charlotte Cushman as Romeo, 1855. From *The Illustrated London News*, 1855.

196 The first production of Dion Boucicault's *The Corsican Brothers* (an adaptation of *Les Frères Corses* by Dumas *père*) in 1852. Enthoven Collection, Victoria and Albert Museum, London.

197 Edwin Forrest as Spartacus in *The Gladiator*, by Robert M. Bird (1806–54), produced in New York in 1831. This shows the London production of 1836. Enthoven Collection, Victoria and Albert Museum, London.

198 A scene from *The Octoroon; or, Life in Louisiana*, by Dion Boucicault. Enthoven Collection, Victoria and Albert Museum, London.

199 Mrs John Drew as Mrs Malaprop in Sheridan's *The Rivals*. Theatre Collection, London, Harvard University.

200 Joseph Jefferson the Third as Rip Van Winkle. Theatre Collection, Harvard University.

201 Charlotte Crabtree (Lotta) as Little Nell in a dramatization by John Brougham (1810–80) of Dickens' *Old Curiosity Shop* (1867), in which she also played 'The Marchioness'. Theatre Collection, Harvard University.

202 John Drew and Ada Rehan in *The Railroad of Love*, adapted by Augustin Daly from a German play, *Goldfische*, and first produced at Daly's Theatre, New York, in 1887, and at the Gaiety in London in the same year. Theatre Collection, Harvard University.

203 Fred Terry in *Henry of Navarre*, by William Devereux.

204 Kate and Ellen Bateman in *The Young Couple*, 1851; an engraving by H. Singleton. Enthoven Collection, Victoria and Albert Museum, London.

205 Henry Irving in *The Bells* by Leopold Lewis. *The Bells* was several times revived, and in 1968 was produced with Marius Goring as Mathias. Enthoven Collection, Victoria and Albert Museum, London.

206 John Martin-Harvey as Sidney Carton in *The Only Way*, 1899, the part in which he was constantly forced by an adoring public to re-appear though he was also excellent in Shakespearean and other roles. Enthoven Collection, Victoria and Albert Museum, London.

207 Irving (*see Ill. 205*) and Ellen Terry as Iachimo and Imogen in *Cymbeline*, 1896. In her *Story of My Life* (1908) Ellen Terry says a great deal about her preparations for playing this part, and it also occasioned some interesting letters to her from Shaw, reprinted in their *Correspondence* (1949). Enthoven Collection, Victoria and Albert Museum, London.

208 Johnston Forbes-Robertson as Hamlet, at the Lyceum, London, 1897.

209 A scene from *The Ticket-of-Leave Man* by Tom Taylor, based on a French tale, and first produced at the Olympic, London, 1863. Enthoven Collection, Victoria and Albert Museum, London.

210 Squire Bancroft and Marie Wilton in *Society* by Tom Robertson (1829–71) at the Prince of Wales's Theatre, 1865. This theatre, formerly the Regency (*see Ill. 117*), had fallen into disrepair, and was nicknamed 'The Dust Hole'. Renovated and redecorated, it became one of the most popular and successful theatres in London. The Bancrofts remained there until 1880, when they moved to the Haymarket. The site is now occupied by the Scala Theatre. Enthoven Collection, Victoria and Albert Museum, London.

211 George Alexander and Allan Aynesworth in Oscar Wilde's *The Importance of Being Earnest*, 1895. Enthoven Collection, Victoria and Albert Museum, London.

212 Sarah Bernhardt and Mrs Patrick Campbell as Pelléas and Mélisande in the play of that name by Maurice Maeterlinck (1862–1949). In this 1904 production Mrs Patrick Campbell, who had played the part in English in 1898, played in French. Enthoven Collection, Victoria and Albert Museum, London.

213 Eleonora Duse in an Italian version of *Die Heimat*, by Hermann Sudermann (1857–1928). Enthoven Collection, Victoria and Albert Museum, London.

214 Marie Lloyd. Enthoven Collection, Victoria and Albert Museum, London.

215 George Robey. Unlike most music-hall comedians, he essayed the legitimate stage, appearing with success as Menelaus in *Helen* in 1932 and as Falstaff in *Henry IV, Part I*, in 1935. Enthoven Collection, Victoria and Albert Museum, London.

216 A private reading of *Les Avariés* by its author, Eugène Brieux, in 1901. The play, like Ibsen's *Ghosts*, dealt with the problem of venereal disease in modern society, and was banned for over a year. As *Damaged Goods*, it was publicly performed in London in 1917. Enthoven Collection, Victoria and Albert Museum, London.

217 A scene from *Little Eyolf* by Henrik Ibsen, 1896. The trans-

lation was by William Archer. Elizabeth Robins, who played Asta, for many years held all the stage rights in Ibsen's plays in their English translations, and was instrumental in arranging their first productions in London. Enthoven Collection, Victoria and Albert Museum, London.

218 Richard Mansfield in The Devil's Disciple by George Bernard Shaw (1856–1950). Mansfield was famous in romantic roles, but was sympathetic to the 'new drama', playing Peer Gynt for the first time in English in 1906, and Bluntschli in Arms and the Man (the first of Shaw's plays to be seen in the United States) in 1894. Theatre Collection, New York Public Library.

219 Sybil Thorndike as Saint Joan. The première of Shaw's play was given in New York at the Garrick Theatre under the auspices of the Theatre Guild in 1923. Enthoven Collection, Victoria and Albert Museum, London.

220 William Poel's production of Hamlet, 1900. He had already produced the play, using the text of the First Quarto (which was also used here) in 1881 at the St George's Hall.

221 The Moscow Art Theatre's production of The Lower Depths by Maxim Gorki, 1902.

222 A scene from Shaw's Androcles and the Lion. The costumes and scenery were by Albert Rutherston. Enthoven Collection, Victoria and Albert Museum, London.

223 Chekhov (1860–1904) reading The Seagull to the company of the Moscow Art Theatre. This play, the first of Chekhov's to be done in English, was first produced in 1896 at the Alexandrinsky Theatre in St Petersburg (now the Pushkin in Leningrad) but was a failure. It needed the youth and vitality of the Moscow Art Theatre to bring it to life.

224 Ernesto Rossi as Hamlet, in a version by Rosconia. Rossi himself translated Julius Caesar into Italian, and was the first Italian actor to play Othello. Enthoven Collection, Victoria and Albert Museum, London.

225 A scene from Six Characters in Search of an Author by Luigi Pirandello (1867–1936). Enthoven Collection, Victoria and Albert Museum, London.

226 A set for Macbeth (I. 3) by Edward Gordon Craig, for a production in New York in 1928. Reproduced by courtesy of the Trustees of the E. Gordon Craig Estate.

227 A set by Adolphe Appia for Ibsen's Little Eyolf. From the original in the Appia Archives, Swiss Theatre Collection, Bern, reproduced by permission of the Curator, Dr Edmond Stadler.

228 The set for Act II of Ibsen's Kongsemnerne (The Crown Pretenders), by Gordon Craig, for a production of the play in 1926, directed by Johannes Poulsen, at the Danish Royal Theatre in Copenhagen. It was Craig's last direct contact with the living theatre. Reproduced by courtesy of the Trustees of the E. Gordon Craig Estate.

229 A scene from a Japanese Noh play, The Lady Aoi, London, 1967.

230 A kyogen, or comic interlude, The Tied Servants, London, 1967.

231 An eighteenth-century print of a Japanese kabuki theatre. British Museum.

232 A modern kabuki play, Kanjinchō, Tokyo, 1960.

233 A scene from a Chinese play.

234 The heroine in a Chinese play.

235 Mei Lan-Fang in one of his female parts.

236 A scene from the American production of Desire Under the Elms, by Eugene O'Neill, in a set by Robert Edmond Jones (1887–1954). The play was seen in London at the Gate Theatre in 1931. Theatre Collection, Harvard University.

237 A production of The Forest, by A.N. Ostrovsky (1823–86), directed and designed by V.E. Meyerhold.

238 The setting for O'Neill's Dynamo (1929), designed by Lee Simonson. The set clearly shows the influence of Meyerhold's reforms (see Ill. 237), and is based on the interior of the power-house in Stevenson, Conn. Vandamm Collection, Theatre Collection, New York Public Library.

239 The Miracle, by Volmöller, produced at Olympia by Max Reinhardt in 1911. The vast crowds assembled for this production, the relationship between actors and audience, and the general lay-out of the various acting-areas, are all strongly reminiscent of what we know of the productions of the great Miracle plays in the Middle Ages. Enthoven Collection, Victoria and Albert Museum, London.

240 A scene from Le Chien du Jardinier, a French version by Georges Neveux of a play by Lope de Vega, a light-hearted comedy of intrigue in which Madeleine Renaud appeared with her husband Jean-Louis Barrault.

241 Louis Jouvet as Molière's Tartuffe.

242 King Lear at the Shakespeare Memorial Theatre, Stratford-upon-Avon, 1937, designed and produced by Theodore Komisarjevsky (1882–1954), a Russian-born actor and director who made a great reputation in England and eventually settled in the United States. By permission of the Governors of the Royal Shakespeare Theatre, Stratford-upon-Avon.

243 The setting for O'Neill's Mourning Becomes Electra, by Robert Edmond Jones (see also Ill. 236).

244 Alfred Lunt and Lynn Fontanne in S.N. Behrman's adaptation of Amphitryon 38, by Jean Giraudoux. It was given

its title because the author reckoned it was the thirty-eighth dramatization of the Alkmena story, first used by Plautus, and later by Molière. Vandamm Collection, Theatre Collection, New York Public Library.

245 John Gielgud as Hamlet, 1934. Although Gielgud rose to the top of his profession as a player of Shakespearean parts, he has appeared in a number of modern plays and has also made a name for himself as a director. Costume by Motley (see Ills. 246–7).

246–7 Costume designs by Motley for Michael Redgrave as Antony in *Antony and Cleopatra*, and Marius Goring as Richard III. Motley were a young firm of designers consisting of two sisters, Sophie and Margaret Harris, and Elizabeth Montgomery. By permission of the Governors of the Royal Shakespeare Theatre, Stratford-upon-Avon.

248 Laurence Olivier in Congreve's *Love for Love*, 1965.

249 Peggy Ashcroft and George Devine in Ibsen's *Hedda Gabler* (1890) at the Lyric Theatre, Hammersmith, in 1954, in an adaptation by Max Faber, directed by Peter Ashmore.

250 Edith Evans in *The Dark is Light Enough*, by Christopher Fry, 1954. Fry's earlier successes in London were *The Lady's Not for Burning* at the Globe in 1949, and *Venus Observed* at the St James's Theatre in 1950.

251 *Ring Round the Moon,* a translation by Christopher Fry of *L'Invitation au Château*, by Jean Anouilh, first produced at the Théâtre de l'Atelier in 1947, with settings and costumes by André Barsacq.

252 The last scene in *Macbeth* – the recognition of Malcolm (played by Ian Richardson) as King – in the 1967 production at the Royal Shakespeare Theatre, Stratford-upon-Avon, directed by Peter Hall.

253 The Berliner Ensemble in *The Days of the Commune* by Bertolt Brecht.

254 The final scene from *The Royal Hunt of the Sun*, by Peter Shaffer, London, 1964. The setting was by Michael Annals, and the music by Marc Wilkinson. The play, previously seen on the open stage of the Chichester Festival Theatre, was produced by John Dexter and Desmond O'Donovan.

255 Costume designs by Peter Rice for *The Beaux' Stratagem*, by George Farquhar, revived at the Chichester Festival Theatre in 1967 with Fenella Fielding as Mrs Sullen. The part was first played in 1707 by Anne Oldfield (1683–1730), and in a revival at the Lyric Hammersmith in 1927, by Edith Evans. Reproduced by kind permission of the Wright Hepburn Gallery.

256 A design by David Hockney for the 1966 London production of *Ubu Roi*, by Alfred

Jarry (1873–1907). Translated and directed by Iain Cuthbertson. Jarry's theory of 'pataphysics' – 'the science of imaginary solutions' – is the basis of the Theatre of the Absurd. By kind permission of the Kasmin Gallery.

257 *Waiting for Godot*, the English version of *En attendant Godot*, by Samuel Beckett, Arts Theatre, London, 1955.

258 A scene from *Who's Afraid of Virginia Woolf?* by Edward Albee, London 1962.

259 A scene from *My Fair Lady*. In the original New York production, Professor Higgins was played by Rex Harrison and Eliza Doolittle by Julie Andrews, who also appeared in these parts at Drury Lane in 1958. The production in both cases was by Moss Hart.

260 The interior of the Mermaid Theatre, Blackfriars, London, opened in May 1959.

261 The stage of the Shakespearean Festival Theatre at Stratford, Ontario. This replaced an earlier tent-like building erected in 1952, and opened in 1957.

262 A set by the Czech scene-designer Josef Svoboda for a production of Sophocles' *Oedipus Rex* at the Prague National Theatre in 1963. The steps, which had movable sections that could be raised to form rostrums, provided a perfect setting for the chorus and principal actors.

Select Bibliography

Reference Works

The Oxford Companion to the Theatre, 3rd edn, ed. Phyllis Hartnoll, London and New York 1967. An encyclopaedia of world theatre.

The Penguin Dictionary of the Theatre, John Russell Taylor, London and New York 1966. Excellent for the modern period, and for information on first productions of well-known plays.

A Shakespeare Encyclopaedia, ed. O.J. Campbell and E.G. Quinn, New York and London 1967. Contains much that would be of interest to all theatregoers, including biographies of leading actors and directors up to modern times, of many of Shakespeare's contemporaries, and of theatre critics and historians through the ages.

The Theatre Handbook and Digest of Plays, Bernard Sobel, 1950. Useful for American material, particularly summaries of play-plots, and for its feature articles on subjects of theatrical interest.

Who's Who in the Theatre, ed. Freda Gay, London 1967. The fourteen editions of this invaluable handbook contain biographical material on actors, dramatists and producers, play-bills of London productions, and related information on long runs, dates of revivals, theatrical families, etc. Some editions contain photographs of actors and productions.

The Biographical Encyclopaedia and Who's Who of the American Theatre, ed. Walter Rigdon, New York 1966. Covers a wide range of theatrical material relating to the United States.

Enciclopedia dello Spettacolo, 9 vols and an Appendix, Rome, 1954–64. Lavishly illustrated.

Illustrated General Histories

G. Altman, etc., *Theater Pictorial*, Berkeley, California 1953.

O.G. Brockett, *The Theatre*, London 1964.

S.W. Cheney, *The Theatre. Three Thousand Years of Drama, Acting and Stagecraft*, New York 1959.

G. Freedley and J.A. Reeves, *A History of the Theatre*, New York 1941.

K. Macgowan and W. Melnitz, *The Living Stage*, New York 1955.

A. Nicoll, *The Development of the Theatre*, 4th edn, London 1958.

T. Prideaux, *World Theatre in Pictures*, Philadelphia 1953.

See also L. Dubech's *Histoire générale illustrée du théâtre*, 5 vols, Paris 1931–4, and H. Kindermann's *Theatergeschichte Europas*, Vienna 1957 – (8 vols published so far).

Technical Studies

L. Barton, *Historic Costume for the Stage*, London and Boston (Mass.) 1949.

F. Bentham, *Stage Lighting*, London 1955.

T. Cole and H.K. Chinoy (eds), *Actors·on Acting, an Anthology*, New York 1949, London 1952.

E.G. Craig, *On the Art of the Theatre*, London and New York 1956.

H.H. Hensen, *Costume Cavalcade*, London 1956.

H. Hunt, *The Director in the Theatre*, London 1954.

S. Joseph, *Scene Painting and Design*, London 1964.

G.R. Kernodle, *From Art to Theatre, Form and Convention in the Renaissance*, Chicago 1943.

J. Laver, *Costume in the Theatre*, London 1964.

S.R. McCandless, *A Method of Lighting the Stage*, 3rd edn, New York 1947.

J. Mielziner, *Designing for the Theatre*, New York 1965.

R. Southern, *The Seven Ages of the Theatre*, London 1962.

K. Stanislavsky, *The Stanislavsky System, the Professional training of an Actor*, New York 1965, London 1966.

F.P. Walkup, *Dressing the Part, a History of Costume for the Theatre*, London 1959.

Further Reading

Peter Arnott, *An Introduction to the Greek Theatre*, London 1961.

D. Blum, *Great Stars of the American Stage, a Pictorial Record*, New York 1952.

D. Ewen, *The Complete Book of the American Theatre*, New York and London 1959.

B. Hewett, *Theatre USA, 1668–1957*, New York 1959.

A. Clunes, *The British Theatre*, London 1964.

W.A. Darlington, *The Actor and his Audience*, London 1949.

R. Mander and J. Mitchenson, *A Picture History of British Theatre*, London 1957.

283

I. Brown, *How Shakespeare Spent the Day*, London 1963.

M. Chute, *Shakespeare of London*, New York 1944, London 1951.

F.E. Halliday, *Shakespeare, a pictorial biography*, London 1956.

J. Kott, *Shakespeare our Contemporary*, London 1964.

C.W. Hodges, *The Globe Restored*, London 1953.

A.C. Sprague, *Shakespeare and the Actors, 1660–1905*, Cambridge (Mass.) 1944.

J. Wain, *The Living World of Shakespeare, a Playgoer's Guide*, London 1964.

P.L. Duchartre, *The Italian Comedy*, London and New York 1929.

K.M. Lea, *Italian Popular Comedy*, 2 vols, Oxford 1963.

A. Nicoll, *The World of Harlequin*, Cambridge 1963.

A. Niklaus, *Harlequin Phoenix*, London 1956.

A.E. Wilson, *The Story of Pantomime*, London 1949.

N.A. Gorchakov, *The Theatre in Soviet Russia*, Columbia and London 1958.

V. Nemirovich-Danchenko, *My Life in the Russian Theatre*, London and Boston (Mass.) 1936.

K. Stanislavsky, *My Life in Art*, London 1962.

B.V. Vareke, *A History of the Russian Theatre*, New York 1951.

J. Chen, *The Chinese Theatre*, London 1949.

A.C. Scott, *The Classical Theatre of China*, London 1957.

F. Bowers, *Japanese Theatre*, New York and London 1956.

E. Ernst, *The Kabuki Theatre*, London 1956.

A.D. Waley, *The No Plays of Japan*, London 1950.

M.R. Anand, *The Indian Theatre*, London 1950.

B. Gargi, *The Theatre in India*, New York 1962.

W. And, *A History of Theatre and Popular Entertainment in Turkey*, Ankara 1963.

Index